THE PERFORMANCE CHALLENGE

Other Books by Jerry W. Gilley

Strategically Integrated HRD (co-author)
Improving HRD Practice
Stop Managing, Start Coaching! (co-author)
Internal Consulting for HRD Professionals (co-author)
Marketing HRD within Organizations (co-author)
Principles of HRD (co-author)

Other Books by Nathaniel W. Boughton

Stop Managing, Start Coaching! (co-author)

Other Books by Ann Maycunich

Strategically Integrated HRD (co-author)

THE
PERFORMANCE
CHALLENGE

Developing Management Systems to
Make Employees Your Organization's
Greatest Asset

JERRY W. GILLEY
NATHANIEL W. BOUGHTON
ANN MAYCUNICH

PERSEUS BOOKS
Cambridge, Massachusetts

Library of Congress Catalog Card Number: 99-068001

ISBN 0-7382-0161-8

Copyright © 1999 Jerry W. Gilley, Nathaniel W. Boughton, and Ann Maycunich

Cover design by Suzanne Heiser
Text design by Nighthawk Design
Set in 10.5/13-point Janson by Nighthawk Design

Perseus Books is a member of the Perseus Books Group.

3   4   5   6   7   8   9   10——03   02   01
First paperback printing, December 1999

Perseus Books are available at special discounts for bulk purchases in the U.S. by corporations, institutions, and other organizations. For more information, please contact the Special Markets Department at HarperCollins Publishers, 10 East 53rd Street, New York, NY 10022, or call 1-212-207-7528.

Find us on the World Wide Web at http://www.perseusbooks.com

Contents

Figures

Acknowledgments

For being a constant source of inspiration I would like to thank C. Shannon Gilley and Melissa G. Gilley, my daughters. Thank you for your love, affection, support, and patience as we grew up together. I will always remember the twinkle in your eyes, scrapes on your knees, your tears of sadness, and your radiant smiles. You have both become beautiful women of whom I am proud. Your spirits are always with me.

I am thankful for the partnership I have shared with Nathaniel W. Boughton and Ann Maycunich during this project. Thank you for your perseverance, dedication, and expertise.

Jerry W. Gilley

To the women in my life; my mother, Nancy, Bailey, and Wyllie for making my dreams come true . . . and to Jerry for opening doors. Thank you.

Nathaniel W. Boughton

The greatest accomplishments in my life have been largely due to the inspiration and support of my family and friends. I thank my parents, Connie and Ken Maycunich, sisters Jen and Therese, and my grandmother, Ann Martin, for a lifetime of love and adventure.

Special friends Marianne and Chris Diedrich, Lynn and Tim Drayton, and Ann and Sig Nowak have made a difference in my life and are forever in my heart. Finally, I'm particularly grateful to Jerry W. Gilley for his inspiration, wisdom, contrariness, and pursuit of excellence—I'm proud to be his friend.

Ann Maycunich

THE PERFORMANCE CHALLENGE

Chapter 1

WHY ORGANIZATIONS AND EMPLOYEES FAIL TO ACHIEVE DESIRED RESULTS

Many organizations have failed miserably in achieving the results required of them. When these organizations are examined closely, one common characteristic surfaces: they can talk the talk, but can't walk the walk. In other words, they have well-written, meaningful mission statements and strategic plans that sound wonderful on paper but are ineffective in helping these organizations make critical, lasting, viable decisions. These same organizations boast that "their employees are their greatest asset," or "their employees are their most valuable resource." In reality, nothing could be further from the truth.

Another common characteristic of organizations that fail to achieve satisfactory results is their inability to secure employee commitment and buy-in to their strategic business goals and objectives. While these organizations will admit that every employee needs to understand how her or his efforts affect business results, few adequately communicate employees' personal responsibility in helping meet organizational goals. Perhaps this is compounded by the rather secretive process that organizations use when drafting strategic business goals and objectives. Closed-door meetings of senior executives identify specific business targets that are then communicated to the rank and file without explanation as to how each employee's contribution will aid in the achievement of corporate goals. Some organizations produce expensive posters and brochures, which are distributed to employees in an attempt to communicate the company's mission. Unfortunately, employees just see fancy words and wasted money rather than gain an understanding of their role in helping the organization achieve its needed results.

Many organizations believe that employees are easily replaced. Consequently, they develop policies and procedures that demonstrate a revolving door philosophy toward human resources. When this philosophy predominates, managers' treatment of employees lacks dignity and respect due to the belief that people are disposable and that an abundant quantity of qualified replacements exists. In some circumstances, employees *are* inadequately prepared to perform the activities necessary to produce acceptable business results; however, an overall callous organizational attitude further compounds an already bad situation, which can lead to costly turnover. Furthermore, employee turnover disrupts the organization, its managers, and its employees, possibly damaging individuals due to the traumatic nature of these experiences.

An attitude of corporate indifference, which Gilley (1998) refers to as Pontius Pilate management, exonerates managers from the responsibility of developing and mentoring employees. He contends this philosophy is based on the belief that managers can "wash their hands of any responsibility for their own actions and decisions" and that employees who fail to meet expectations can be fired. When this attitude prevails, managers are often autocratic and difficult to work with. They firmly believe a buyer's market exists and that a vast number of individuals are looking for work. If current employees are unhappy or don't like their circumstances, they can work elsewhere. An indifferent attitude such as this kills employee morale and severely limits loyalty and commitment.

Some organizations fail to achieve satisfactory results due to lack of a strategic vision of the future. As a result, they tend to meander into fields far from the organization's central core (frequently due to unwise mergers and acquisitions). Over time, organizations find themselves far off course, aimlessly adrift, and hopelessly lost in competitive seas. They unknowingly fall victim to the Buddhist aphorism that if you don't know where you're going, any road will get you there.

Organizations lacking strategic vision often fall victim to management fads, wasting thousands of dollars on training programs and activities designed to improve every possible organizational ill. Without clear direction, organizations often accept any solution that has the potential of improving their effectiveness. A "quick fix" mentality such as this prohibits serious deliberation regarding a long-term, strategic approach to improving organizational efficiency and effectiveness.

Many organizations fail to achieve their desired results due to an inability to adjust to ever-changing conditions. According to Patterson (1997), *resilience* is the capacity of an organization and its members to absorb change without draining the organization's or its employees' energies. He believes that resilience is like a personal energy account, including such things as time, thought, and effort spent on adjusting to change. Thus, resilience is the price organizations pay for change in their attempts to adapt and adjust to it appropriately.

Many organizations are unable to adapt to change because they maintain faulty assumptions related to change activities. Among these are that organizations are rationally functioning systems that can adjust systematically to changing conditions. This is simply not the case because organizations operate in their own best interests—which may or may not be rational. Another faulty assumption is that organizations can achieve long-term, systematic change with short-term leadership. Under these conditions, organizations opt to employ outside consulting firms to initiate long-term change instead of using the management team that must live with the ultimate decisions. Finally, organizations mistakenly believe that systematic change can occur without creating conflict in the system. Organizations remain unrealistic about the amount of conflict that occurs as a result of change, naively expecting change to be accepted wholeheartedly by employees.

These are but a few of the reasons why organizations do not achieve their desired results. Each is an example of how organizations fail at the strategic or macro level. The most common intervention used to help organizations facing this kind of problem is strategic planning. According to Gilley and Maycunich (1998), strategic planning is a forward-thinking process that helps organizational leaders shape the future via intelligent, informed, innovative actions. They believe that strategic planning provides purpose and direction to an organization by allowing it to ascertain, in advance, what it wishes to accomplish and how. Strategic planning also permits employees, managers, and executives to participate in decision making, thus allowing all to personally impact the organization's future. The primary purpose of strategic planning is to continually re-create and reinvent organizations by helping them establish a new vision and purpose. Consequently, strategic planning can enhance organizational effectiveness by charting a new course for the organization.

THE PERFORMANCE CHALLENGE

When organizations are confronted with a strategic or macro-level problem, strategic planning provides an excellent intervention. However, the goal of every organization is to make money for its owners or stockholders. This proves to be an extremely difficult task unless organizations discover ways to improve the efficiency and effectiveness of their operations. One way of accomplishing this is to secure better results from each and every employee within the organization. Consequently, the dilemma facing most organizations is that they simply do not know how to manage performance, develop people, and create systems and techniques that enhance organizational effectiveness—which is the focus of this book. In short, organizations must discover ways of transforming everyday employees into high performers who are their greatest assets.

A visit to any local bookstore demonstrates numerous attempts to overcome the performance challenge, which can be a simple but everdaunting problem. Among the myriad of books written, few have laid out a comprehensive, systematic approach to addressing the performance challenge. Many qualified, well-meaning authors have addressed the corporate performance challenge in piecemeal fashion as evidenced by masterpieces on topics such as:

- the client-centered organization
- reengineering
- the consultative approach to management
- coaching principles
- performance appraisal and review
- training and development
- compensation and reward systems

Separately, these books address only one, possibly two, of the major components required to improve employee and organizational performance. Collectively they may help organizations address the performance challenge while failing to provide a systematic, organized, and comprehensive approach.

THE PERFORMANCE ALIGNMENT PROCESS

The performance challenge facing every organization is to develop management systems that make employees the organization's greatest asset. To successfully reach this pinnacle, an organization must design, develop, and implement a *performance alignment process* intended to improve its performance and competitiveness—in other words, a process that addresses the performance challenge. According to Gilley (1998), this process must incorporate an organization-wide approach that combines the entire performance improvement process into one cohesive operating system. He further contends that an organization-wide performance alignment process links performance to compensation and rewards, the organization's strategic business goals and objectives, and client needs and expectations.

The performance alignment process consists of seven separate but interrelated steps:

Step 1: Conducting Stakeholder Valuation
Step 2: Improving Job Design
Step 3: Establishing Synergistic Relationships
Step 4: Applying Performance Coaching
Step 5: Conducting Developmental Evaluations
Step 6: Creating Performance Growth and Development Plans
Step 7: Linking Compensation and Rewards to Performance Growth and Development

Each builds on the others, forming a systematic and comprehensive approach to addressing the performance challenge (Figure 1.1). This approach separates performance alignment into two distinct phases. Steps 1 and 2 are the responsibility of the *organization;* steps 3 through 7 are the responsibility of *managers and employees.* This approach is predicated on the belief that employees are the center of influence that drive business results—which means they need to understand and align their performance with the organization's strategic business goals and objectives.

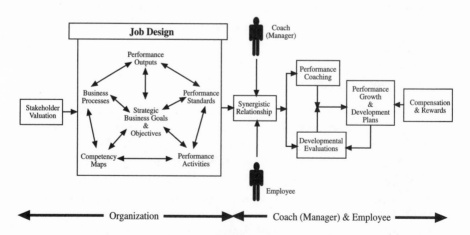

Figure 1.1 Performance Alignment Model

Step 1: Conducting Stakeholder Valuation

It is impossible for an organization to achieve desired business results without identifying its clients' needs and expectations. Organizations must actively seek to understand their stakeholders and the values that they place on the products and services they receive. Most employees have little or no direct contact with *external* clients, which prevents them from fully appreciating client needs and expectations. Conversely, employees have a great deal of interaction with internal clients as they go about their everyday roles and responsibilities. Unfortunately, few employees view their co-workers as *internal* clients. As a result, they fail to solicit their co-workers' input, recommendations, and suggestions.

Organizations must design strategies that allow each employee to understand his or her impact on both internal and external clients. A number of strategies such as cross-functional training, cross-functional teaming, and interdepartmental internships can be used.

Once employees clearly understand how clients think, they are able to identify needs and provide solutions. The organization is now driving on a highway to long-term success. Organizations will then have a more effective, productive workforce through the alignment of employees to clients' needs and expectations.

Identifying client needs and expectations can be accomplished through the process of stakeholder valuation, which serves as a reality test for organizations and their managers. In other words, client needs and expectations drive the organization's efforts to deliver value to clients (see Chapter 2). This information is obtainable through surveys, focus groups, and interviews. Consequently, stakeholder valuation serves as the genesis of the performance alignment process. This step must be completed prior to implementing step 2.

Step 2: Improving Job Design

At the core of the job design process are strategic business goals and objectives of the organization. Jobs are designed to help the organization achieve its most important objective—desired business results. These become the targets for the entire performance alignment process.

While many employees are unaware of the strategic business goals and objectives of their organization, these are readily available and represent the criteria used in measuring the entire organization's success. The most common examples of strategic business goals and objectives include sales revenue, market share, and profit target. They can also include competitive position, market projections, and quality and efficiency measures.

Once the organization's strategic business goals and objectives have been identified, the job design process can begin. This process consists of five interdependent functions used to produce a product or service. They include:

1. business processes
2. performance outputs
3. performance standards
4. performance activities
5. competency maps (see Chapter 3)

By examining each of these five steps and determining their dependencies, organizations identify efficiencies that enable them to be more profitable and competitive. In fact, it could be said that an organization is only as efficient and effective as its job designs.

Organizations can also use this five-step process to determine the reason they fail to achieve their desired strategic business goals and objectives. Reshaping, reorganizing, redefining, and replacing job designs may be in order.

Step 3: Establishing Synergistic Relationships

Organizations cannot possibly address the performance challenge without establishing positive working relationships between managers and employees—ones that enhance employee commitment to improving performance and quality, and increasing productivity and organizational results (Gilley & Boughton, 1996). Positive relationships produce a synergy between managers and employees (see Chapter 4). Let's examine this definition and its separate parts.

A "positive working relationship" is one that benefits all parties, allowing each to receive the specific outcomes they desire. Such a relationship is professional, enabling managers and employees to work closely together. Gilley and Boughton (1996) believe that "enhancing employee commitment" refers to an employee's willingness to make personal sacrifices to reach her or his team, department, and organizational goals. They believe that in order to enhance commitment, managers must clarify the goals of the team, department, and organization, provide the training necessary to enhance the competencies required, and allow greater employee influence in decision making. In exchange for their enhanced commitment, managers should reward employees appropriately (see Chapter 8). Managers can improve performance and quality, and increase productivity and organizational results by creating work environments dedicated to continuous improvement (see Chapter 7). It is our contention that employees will influence the organization's outcomes if they are treated and perform like owners. This can only be achieved when managers and employees have established a synergistic relationship.

Step 4: Applying Performance Coaching

One of the most critical components of the performance challenge is to understand the manager's role in transforming employees into the organization's greatest asset. Without a doubt, the most common and debilitating problem facing organizations today is quality (or lack thereof) of management. Every organization harbors managers who are indifferent toward their employees, possess superior attitudes, and consider employees as something to use and abuse. Unfortunately, many managers have poor listening, feedback, and interpersonal relationship skills, can't produce a positive relationship with their employees, and cannot delegate, develop their employees, conduct performance appraisals, or establish priorities. Some of these managers criticize their employees' efforts, creating work environments characterized by fear and paranoia. When these conditions are allowed to continue, organizations are encouraging and fostering *managerial malpractice* (Gilley & Boughton, 1996). Managerial malpractice is simply encouraging and supporting practices that enable unprofessional, unproductive, and incompetent managers to remain with an organization. Determining if such an environment exists is possible by examining whether the organization practices the following:

1. keeping managers who are not good at getting results from people
2. promoting people to management roles before determining their "managerial aptitude"
3. selecting new managers because they are the best performers or producers without regard for their people skills
4. spending valuable time "fixing" managerial incompetence instead of hiring qualified managers
5. keeping managers who preach the importance of teamwork, yet reward those individuals who stand out in the crowd
6. allowing managers to say one thing and do another (Gilley & Boughton, 1996, p. 1)

If a majority of these symptoms exist within the organization, it is guilty of managerial malpractice. The solution is simple: select managers for their people skills and hold them accountable for securing results through people. This requires managers to become involved with their employees by establishing rapport and encouraging face-to-face communications.

Organizations have allowed managerial malpractice to exist far too long. Managerial malpractice frustrates employees and negatively impacts productivity and organizational effectiveness. Organizations must learn how to transform managers into performance coaches in order to overcome managerial malpractice. Performance coaching is a series of one-to-one exchanges between managers and their employees; it is a person-centered management process used to help solve problems, improve performance, and get results. Performance coaching requires managers to shift constantly from one role to another; training, counseling, confronting, and mentoring. Each role enhances employees' self-esteem, and helps the organization achieve better business results.

Step 5: Conducting Developmental Evaluations

Most organizations have some kind of annual performance appraisal process designed to provide performance coaches with an opportunity to judge the adequacy and quality of employee performance and to create performance improvement and development plans to enhance performance. Developmental evaluations should be used to determine whether employees are demonstrating acceptable performance activities (Gilley, 1998) and generating outputs that meet or exceed performance standards. Developmental evaluations should also be used to determine whether the needs and expectations of internal and external clients have been satisfied; assess employees' strengths and weaknesses by comparing their competencies against job requirements; examine how employee performance is helping the organization achieve its strategic business goals and objectives; and design acceptable performance activities (Gilley, 1998). Regardless of their use, developmental evaluations are an excellent tool when assessing employee performance and making recommendations for improvement (see Chapter 6).

Step 6: Creating Performance Growth and Development Plans

The primary purposes of developmental evaluations are for performance coaches to identify the strengths and weaknesses of their employees and to discuss ways of enhancing employee performance growth and development. From this perspective, performance growth and development plans become a long-term strategy instead of a quick fix.

One of managers' biggest temptations is to "fix" their employees rather than discover things that they do well. Consequently, most training and development activities are designed to *fix weaknesses* instead of capitalize on employees' strengths. In Chapter 7, we will discuss the process performance coaches go through in developing areas of expertise that enable employees to maximize their personal productivity. These areas of expertise are based on strengths, not weaknesses. If an employee's areas of expertise produce high levels of performance, it makes sense to focus on these areas. Therefore, performance coaches must develop their employees' strengths and help them manage their weaknesses.

Performance coaches can assist employees in the design, development, and implementation of an outstanding learning acquisition and transfer plan that enhances their growth and development. But unless employees transfer what they learn to the job, it is a complete waste of time, energy, effort, and money. If employees fail to transfer learning to the job, the performance alignment process is utterly destroyed. No other activity is more important to learning transfer.

Learning cannot be translated into value for the organization unless it is applied to the job. Consequently, performance growth and development plans must be designed in such a way that enables employees to apply learning to the job. Furthermore, performance coaches must provide immediate feedback to their employees regarding the application of new knowledge on the job. When this occurs, employees realize the importance of acquiring new knowledge and making the effort to integrate it into their job.

Step 7: Linking Compensation and Rewards to Performance Growth and Development

Performance coaches must establish a clear link between producing positive outcomes and having employees' efforts recognized. According to LeBoeuf (1985), research has shown that the performances that get rewarded and reinforced are repeated. Consequently, organizations are challenged to install compensation and reward systems that build commitment and improve employee motivation. That is, organizations must reward the right things. Once proper compensation and reward systems are in place, performance coaches must link performance enhancement to them (see Chapter 8).

In Chapter 8, the principles of performance enhancement are examined, helping explain why employees behave the way they do. Also examined are seven reward strategies that help performance coaches enhance employee commitment and secure results. They include rewarding:

1. long-term solutions
2. entrepreneurship
3. leadership
4. performance growth and development
5. teamwork and cooperation
6. creativity
7. employee commitment and loyalty

Each of these strategies provides a better understanding of the impact of compensation and rewards on employee and organizational performance. Also examined are several types of rewards that prove successful in enhancing performance.

DEVELOPING LEADERSHIP EFFECTIVENESS

Regardless of the initiative used or strategy employed to improve organizational performance, one element is absolutely essential: effective leadership. Without effective leaders, organizations are doomed to wander forever in the corporate wilderness, helplessly lost, unable to chart a course to sustainable financial success. We contend that effective leaders help organizations redefine and reinvent themselves for the purposes of delivering quality products and services in a timely manner. Thus, another strategy that addresses the performance challenge involves developing leadership effectiveness.

In Chapter 9, we examine four competencies of effective leaders, which include:

- critical reflective skills
- strategic thinking skills
- interpersonal skills
- performance-enhancing skills

Leaders possessing these skills are able to create work environments where employees flourish and strive for excellence. As a result, their organizations more effectively address the performance challenge.

CREATING VIRTUAL TEAMS

Making the transformation from work groups to virtual teams provides another important tactic for addressing the performance challenge (Chapter 10). While work groups are necessary to help the organization achieve desired business results, virtual teams are needed to foster organizational synergy—where leaders and employees work together to improve the harmony and efficiency of the organization. Virtual teams are based on the assumption that employees encounter a higher degree of job-related problems while leaders hold the authority necessary to solve them. Simultaneously, employees have little authority to solve job-related problems while leaders have little knowledge of the problems themselves. Working collaboratively, however, they combine their respective knowledge as well as overcome their collective deficiencies. As a result, leaders and employees work together in addressing the performance challenge and transforming employees into their greatest asset.

PRINCIPLES OF PERFORMANCE IMPROVEMENT

Have you ever wondered why employees behave the way they do? Have you ever wondered why they fail to achieve performance results required of them? We believe that three fundamental principles explain most employee behavior and why organizations fail to secure the results they need or want. The principles include performance/reward disconnect, performance whitewashing, and inspection failure.

Many employees fail to perform adequately because there is a disconnect between their performance and that rewarded by the organization (*performance/reward disconnect*). For example, many organizations have embraced the concept of team building and have spent millions of dollars training their people in the skills, knowledge, and practice of self-directed work teams; however, they continue to compensate their employees for individual performance. This is compounded when bonuses and other financial rewards are given to employees based on their individual contributions rather than those of the team on which they are members. In other words, the performance behaviors that an organization desires are being ignored or punished in the workplace while other behaviors are being rewarded.

Organizations send mixed messages when they: ask for quality work but establish unrealistic deadlines for completion; want projects finished on time but do nothing when a senior manager delays until the last minute to begin a project; or place great emphasis on other outcomes or results but reward those employees who "look" the busiest and work the longest hours. In order to improve organizational performance, a direct correlation should exist between desired performance and rewards received. If people are rewarded for the right performance, the organization will get the right performance. Failure to reward proper performance behavior will lead to undesirable results. That is, the things that get rewarded get done (LeBoeuf, 1985).

Another factor contributing to inappropriate performance occurs when managers treat all performance results the same and fail to communicate which results are the most important—which we refer to as *performance whitewashing*. This behavior confuses employees and causes them to prioritize results according to their own perspectives. Sometimes their performance outcomes are of little value to the organization. If employees are allowed to continue to focus on less important priorities, the organization will not receive the results it needs. However, the problem is not with employees' performance, but with managers' inabilities to prioritize performance outcomes.

In order to correct this problem, managers must focus on the right things. They must determine which results are truly important and which are less so. Once identified, these priorities must be communicated to employees and rewarded accordingly. That is, once a manager has identified employees' highest priorities and rewarded them accordingly, the organization has created a results strategy that will produce positive outcomes.

Many employees fail to produce desired performance outcomes because managers fail to inspect their work (*inspection failure*). Since some managers spend little time reviewing or inspecting employees' outputs, employees are left on their own to produce results they perceive to be important to the organization. Failure to prioritize or inspect performance outputs both lead to the same conclusion: inadequate or disappointing performance and results. In order to overcome the latter problem, managers must link expectations with inspection. This can occur during the performance coaching (Chapter 5) or developmental evaluation (Chapter 6) phases of the performance alignment process. Employees must know what is important to produce and understand that their managers will be inspecting their performance outputs.

Why Employees and Organizations Fail to Achieve Desired Performance Results

One of the best ways of determining the effectiveness of an organization is by examining its employees' performance. If an organization is not achieving its desired business goals and objectives, it could be because employees are not performing adequately. Seven **reasons** explain organizations' failure to achieve desired results (Figure 1.2), and eighteen critical **reasons** detail why employees do not perform adequately (Figure 1.3).

1. Failing to focus on stakeholders' needs (Chapter 2).
2. Failing to link organizational performance to strategic business goals and objectives (Chapter 3).
3. Failing to identify performance breakdowns (Chapter 3).
4. Failing to eliminate managerial malpractice (Chapters 4, 5, 6, 7, & 8).
5. Failing to manage performance (Chapter 5).
6. Failing to encourage employee involvement and support (Chapter 7).
7. Failing to focus on long-term results (Chapter 8).

Figure 1.2 Reasons Why Organizations Fail to Achieve Desired Performance Results

1. They focus on less important activities (Chapter 3).
2. There are barriers and obstacles preventing adequate performance (Chapter 3).
3. Their jobs are poorly designed (Chapter 3).
4. They don't know how to measure or evaluate their performance (Chapter 3).
5. They don't feel safe asking for help (Chapter 4).
6. They are fearful of repercussions for doing their jobs incorrectly (Chapter 4).
7. They don't trust their managers (Chapter 4).
8. They don't have the knowledge or skills to do their jobs (Chapters 5 & 7).
9. They don't know how to do their jobs (Chapter 5).
10. They don't understand their job responsibilities (Chapter 5).
11. They think there is a better way of doing their jobs (Chapters 5 & 6).
12. They are not confronted when they don't perform their jobs correctly (Chapters 5 & 6).
13. They refuse to produce the required performance outputs (Chapters 5 & 6).
14. They think they are doing their jobs correctly (Chapter 6).
15. They have personal problems that prevent them from doing their jobs (Chapter 6).
16. They are not rewarded for doing their jobs (Chapter 8).
17. They are rewarded for doing less important activities (Chapter 8).
18. They are asked to do one thing (i.e., work as a team) but are rewarded for another (individual compensation and bonuses) (Chapter 8).

Figure 1.3 Reasons Why Employees Fail to Achieve Desired Performance Results

Performance Alignment Process	Organizational Failure Reasons	Employee Failure Reasons
Stakeholder Valuation (Chapter 2)	1	
Job Design (Chapter 3)	2 & 3	1, 2, 3, & 4
Synergistic Relationships (Chapter 4)	4	5, 6, & 7
Performance Coaching (Chapter 5)	4 & 5	8, 9, 10, 11, 12, & 13
Developmental Evaluations (Chapter 6)	4	11, 12, 13, 14, & 15
Performance Growth & Development Plans (Chapter 7)	4 & 6	8
Linking Compensation & Rewards to Performance Growth & Development Plans (Chapter 8)	4 & 7	16, 17, & 18

Figure 1.4 Performance Alignment Process and Reasons Why Organizations and Employees Fail to Achieve Performance Results

Applying the performance alignment process provides the organization and managers with a systematic way of addressing each of these organizational and employee problems respectively. We have developed a comprehensive overview of how the performance alignment process can be used to address employee and organizational failures (Figure 1.4). This comprehensive overview will help identify which part of the performance alignment process should be used to isolate and overcome a specific performance failure. Each of these critical **reasons** for inadequate performance will be addressed throughout the remaining chapters as the performance alignment process is explained (see Chapters 2–8).

CONCLUSION

Addressing the performance challenge proves a difficult undertaking requiring cooperation from the organization, its managers, and its employees. One of the best ways of improving organizational and employee performance is by utilizing an organization-wide performance alignment process—one that links client needs and expectations to job design (organization) and the performance improvement process (managers and employees) in such a way as to enhance organizational competitiveness, efficiency, and effectiveness.

Two additional strategies are particularly successful in meeting the performance challenge: developing leadership effectiveness and creating virtual teams. Collectively, these strategies effectively transform employees into an organization's greatest asset.

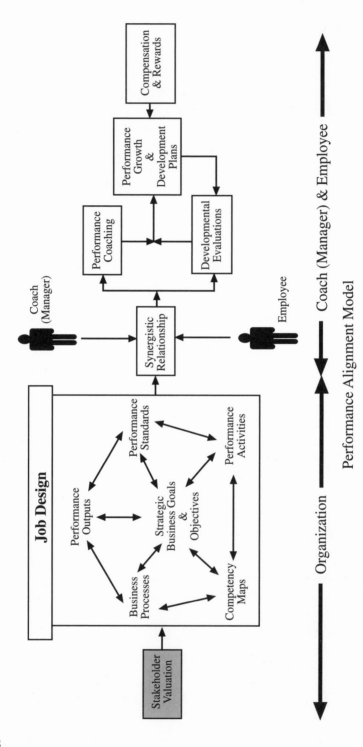

Performance Alignment Model

Chapter 2

CONDUCTING STAKEHOLDER VALUATIONS

Using market research is a classic method for discovering the needs and expectations of those the organization is attempting to serve—its stakeholders (reason 1, see Figure 1.2). But who are stakeholders? Many organizations feel this is an easy question to answer; reality, unfortunately, is somewhat different.

Organizations need to spend a fair amount of time identifying their stakeholders—the ones who must be served. The two types of stakeholders common to most organizations are internal and external. Recently, we worked with the Metropolitan Atlanta Rapid Transit Authority (MARTA) and asked them to identify their stakeholders. One of the managers listed their riders. Our next question was, "How many of you (managers) have direct contact with riders on a daily basis?" Only one out of eighteen participants had direct contact with their riders (customers). Testing this question again, we also asked it of managers at a major communications corporation. The managers were clear who their stakeholders were—their consumers. Again, we asked how many of them had direct contact with their consumers. They indicated less than 20 percent. So, how well do organizations understand the needs and expectations of their stakeholders? And, how can organizations serve people when they don't know what stakeholders need or want?

When stakeholders are successfully identified, an organization clearly has a fundamental advantage over the competition and can increase market share and desired business outcomes as a result. Each employee needs to have a thorough understanding of his or her interaction with different types of stakeholders, both directly and indirectly.

We have created the Stakeholder Valuation model to identify organizational stakeholders (Figure 2.1). The model is divided into two parts, internal and external. Within each of these parts are three components:

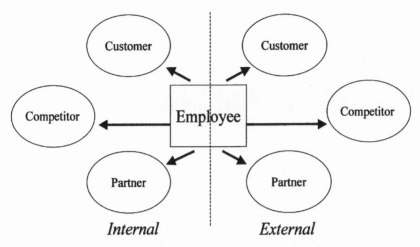

Figure 2.1 Stakeholder Valuation Model

1. customers (consumers and clients)
2. competitors
3. partners

These three components interact continuously and need to be clearly understood by each employee throughout the organization. We'll take a closer look at internal and external stakeholders and the relationship among the three different types of stakeholders.

EXTERNAL STAKEHOLDERS

External stakeholders are those individuals who purchase an organization's products or use their services. They are outside the organization and have something to gain or maintain as a result of using these products or services or having a relationship with the organization. They may be suppliers, joint venture groups, end users, or competitors. Most commonly, external stakeholders consist of customers, partners, and competitors.

External stakeholders engage in the exchange of value between themselves and the organization. That is, external stakeholders are those individuals who have a desire to buy the organization's products and services, and do so by engaging in a process known as exchange, which is the sharing of value between two parties. One party will offer a product or service in exchange for another party's money, time, energy, or effort. If the value received is equal to or greater in importance than the value given, then a positive exchange will occur. Exchange will not occur when one or both parties perceive that they are the recipients of negative value while giving up positive value. Therefore, the needs and expectations of external stakeholders must be identified in order to effectively engage in the exchange process.

Customers

By identifying customers, organizations better focus their products and services to meet their clients' needs and expectations. Thus, it is of paramount importance for organizations to identify the individuals who use their products or services (customer, client, or consumer). This group can be found in the upper-right-hand corner of the Stakeholder Valuation model (Figure 2.1), and has a solid line and arrow leading to it that symbolizes the need for increased employer knowledge and interaction. Organizational identification of external customers is critical.

In the MARTA study, we asked several follow-up questions, which yielded a wealth of information. It was easy to understand that the customer was a rider, but we found that the system had a variety of riders, from those that used the system to commute to and from work or school, to others who used the system for special events. Regardless, each group wanted safe, clean, timely service. Apart from these general statements, the needs and expectations of each group were different; MARTA needed its employees to provide services that met the different needs and expectations of each customer group. If employees treat each customer group the same, service quality diminishes; therefore, having a clear idea of who the organization's external customers are and how to best serve them provides the organization with optimal business opportunities and better results.

Partners

Another critical external stakeholder group consists of partners—those individuals or groups that aid in the design, development, and delivery of products and services to the organization's respective markets. In each and every case, external partners have a financial stake in the success of the organization's products and services.

External partners comprising vertical integration are those stakeholders who directly impact the design, development, and production of organizational products and services. This group can include parts suppliers, original equipment producers, providers of raw materials, or any other group that supplies components to the production of products or services.

External partners that form a horizontal integration of the business are those stakeholders that indirectly impact the support, service, and distribution of products and services. These can include software experts who design a system, the technicians, experts, or consultants that support the business, research and development professionals who design and test products or services, or customer service agents who handle complaints.

Each employee needs to have a complete understanding of the role of external partners on the vertical and horizontal planes, and their impact on business results. This is accomplished by adopting a management philosophy that allows employees to interact with external partners and to develop a keen sense of their importance, needs, and expectations (see Chapter 10). Questions that should be asked regarding this group are:

- How do we identify partners in our industry?
- Are we limited only to those partners with horizontal integration, or should we consider vertical integration as well?
- How will our business be impacted by creating external partnerships?

Competitors

Organizational success often depends on employees' knowledge of the competition and their impact on the business. The most common form of competition is direct. Direct competitors provide the same products or services within the industry as your organization. For example, Coca-Cola and Pepsi, Nike and Reebok, Delta and American Airlines, and Exxon and Mobil are direct competitors of each other, battling viciously for market share every day. Identification and assessment of direct competitors help an organization make appropriate adjustments to remain viable. Employees must be aware of the competitions' advantages and disadvantages in order to adequately and proactively promote or defend your business, products, or services.

When discussing competitors with employees, three elements are key:

- Ask them what they know about the competition—this valuable input is a reservoir of information to be tapped when necessary.

- Involve employees by allowing them to collaborate in decision making (see Chapter 10).
- Include employees in the upward flow of information. Ask for suggestions and recommendations on how to adjust to competitor initiatives.

These three principles provide a dramatic foundation for employees to add value to the organization, and allow organizations to identify ways of improving their products and services, which helps them compete successfully in the worldwide marketplace.

INTERNAL STAKEHOLDERS

Internal stakeholders are difficult for employees to identify and understand, even though they are interacted with on a regular basis. Internal stakeholders consist of customers, partners, and competitors (Figure 2.1). Intuitively, employees understand that they must meet the needs and expectations of these entities, yet they often do a poor job because they rarely view these groups as stakeholders. The problem exists due to employees' lack of understanding of the importance of meeting internal stakeholders' needs and expectations. Consequently, they hold little or no regard for how their actions affect stakeholders (see Chapter 3). To overcome this problem, organizations must first identify appropriate stakeholders, then ascertain their needs and expectations.

Customers

Internal customers consist of individuals or groups that help the organization produce its products or services. They can be found in departments, units, or divisions that provide important human or material resources, performance outputs, or information critical to the execution of performance activities or the delivery of products and services (see Chapter 3). An internal stakeholder may be a department that sells its services within the organization. For example, SeaFirst Bank, the Arthur Anderson Corporation, and Motorola Corporation all have internal corporate universities that provide training. These departments are responsible for generating revenue internally in exchange for training programs and services. Their customers consist of other employees and departments.

Identifying internal customers and their respective needs and expectations is critical as it allows an organization (and its employees) to understand what it must do to meet their demands. Successfully identifying internal customers' needs and expectations allows an organization to anticipate the changes that will impact their results.

When working with ACI's corporate university, we were able to help them identify their internal customers' training needs and budgetary constraints. If ACI's corporate university had not taken this approach, they would not know their internal customers' specific needs or what they would be willing to pay for the opportunity to participate in training. By doing so, ACI's corporate university can offer training programs and services that add value and benefit the organization.

Partners

Internal partners differ from internal customers in that they mutually share in the risks and benefits associated with products and services. An internal partnership consists of two or more groups jointly delivering products or services to internal customers and sharing in both the benefits and risks associated with such ventures. The success of these internal activities depends solely on their mutual cooperation and collaboration. Communications is therefore critical to internal partnerships—without which partners may be going in different directions, thus preventing successful achievement of desired objectives.

Internal partners must identify and communicate their needs and expectations of each other. To guarantee success, internal partners must:

1. Identify all parties involved in the partnership.
2. Identify and communicate the respective needs and expectations of all participants.
3. Allow time for all participants to understand the value of the partnership relationship.
4. Define members' roles and responsibilities within the partnership.
5. Encourage partners to discuss problems or mutually beneficial issues.
6. Establish focus groups made up of partners to ensure a proactive, collaborative approach to problem solving.

This information will help an organization create synergistic relationships and promote mutual sharing of information and ideas.

Securing buy-in from all partnership participants is critical to its success. If employees fail to understand their impact on the partnership, productivity and quality will not improve. Partnership success also depends on anticipating problems. The more employees know about their partners, the more likely they will be able to anticipate problems and respond proactively. Through partnership interaction, employees will learn new skills and gain new information that will help them in future decision making. This creates a "knowledge bank" within the partnership that can be drawn on to resolve problems and achieve desired results.

Taking this relationship to the next logical level, employees become coaches within the partnership, responsible for information sharing, problem resolution, and providing feedback and reinforcement. This critical, collaborative process is instrumental in the success of internal partnerships.

Competitors

Internal competition exists within all organizations, between departments, offices, divisions, or regions. While we rarely consider our internal competitors to be stakeholders, they are indeed because they have something to gain or lose as a result of their interactions within the firm. Unfortunately, most internal competition produces negative interaction and results. A large consulting firm we worked for had seven independent practice areas, each of which had a significant number of clients and tremendous revenue. Each practice area was extremely paranoid about sharing its business internally, feeling they were in constant competition with other organizational practice areas. Their attitude was, "Why share our client base?" As a result, the organization had very few clients to whom they provided more than one service and, therefore, missed many opportunities to cross-sell products or services to clients, which hindered their revenue growth and profitability potential. While far from unusual, organization competition such as this harms business outcomes.

We refer to internal competition as the "silo effect" because departments, divisions, regions, or practices tend to operate within very narrowly defined, windowless silos. Lacking is the opportunity to share information and experiences, or to provide a more integrated approach to satisfying customers' needs and expectations. This self-centered existence ultimately harms the organization and can be extremely detrimental to the bottom line. A competitive environment such as this calls for transformation to a more collaborative, integrated effort.

Three steps may be followed by an organization when creating healthy, collaborative competition:

- Communicate the responsibilities of each practice unit, department, or division to every other practice unit, department, or division.
- Design a cross-functional training activity that demonstrates the varied abilities, skills, and talents brought to the table by different managers and employees.
- Reward leaders and employees for collaborative interaction.

This three-step approach promotes healthy internal interaction and integration, resulting in enhanced efficiency leading to long-term organizational viability.

We recently worked for a financial institution that realized it was unsuccessful in cross-selling its different products and services to external customers. For example, the installment loan department focused only on personal loans, and was not concerned about promoting IRAs, CDs, or financial products offered by other operational units. Other departments, such as customer service, neglected to provide information regarding alternative areas within the financial institution and were only concerned with solving problems within their own narrowly defined niches. In order to help the organization develop a collaborative environment, we met with leaders to discuss the negative outcomes of this competitive environment. Next, we conducted focus groups with staff and identified ways of creating collaborative opportunities. When completed, we designed a training initiative that helped respective groups implement collaborative opportunities. We followed up with additional self-help programs and identified internal coaches to work with employees to help them transfer learning to the job and make certain that a more collaborative approach was being implemented. As a result, the organization instituted a personal service program that allows clients to meet with one employee to open any account. Everyone within the organization is rewarded for the increase in asset and loan growth, instead of only one person or department receiving recognition for individual success.

Some organizations may feel this approach diminishes the positive outcomes of competition. On the contrary, we have found that organizations that adopt a collaborative approach actually increase their return on investment, revenue growth, and profitability. Furthermore, the collaborative approach helps organizations focus their efforts at meeting the needs of each and every internal and external customer. Adherence to the silo (departmental) approach leaves too much information on the table, which eventually permits an organization's external stakeholders (competitors) to take advantage of missed opportunities. Over time, these missed opportunities translate into lost customers.

We have seen a collaborative approach among internal competitors significantly impact organizational business results. Via the collaborative approach, organizations are able to exceed their customers' expectations and increase revenue streams, which ultimately improves profitability and viability.

Another common type of competition exists within an organization when resources are scarce and departments aggressively compete for them. Occasionally, departments compromise with one another in the fight for resources. Unfortunately, this type of compromise can be negative in that, regardless of outcome, both parties lose—which obviously doesn't benefit the organization. Again, organizations need to use a collaborative approach to competition for scarce resources.

Organizations should identify the respective needs of their individual departments and each one's effect on other areas within the firm. This partnership approach provides opportunities to use collaborative techniques.

When departments protect their turf, communications suffer and the organization fails to maximize its business potential. This approach results in a great deal of repetition and overlapping responsibility. When these conditions exist, precious financial resources (often hundreds of thousands of dollars) are wasted as departments ignore necessary change in an effort to avoid losing control of their organizational hierarchy. Consequently, organizational focus on creating collaborative partnerships remains critical. To this end, organizations must brainstorm issues and solutions, integrate all levels of employee involvement, and reward employees for overall organizational success. By using this approach, an organization creates synergy, builds efficient processes that positively impact business results, and becomes more agile in its interactions with stakeholders.

IDENTIFYING STAKEHOLDER NEEDS

Needs are the problems or issues that must be resolved before an organization can reach its business goals and objectives. They are the gaps that must be filled in order for an organization to function effectively and provide value to all stakeholders. The following questions help identify stakeholder needs:

- What is the difference between our current and desired results?
- What are the needs of our customers, partners, and competitors?
- Am I and my staff able to meet these needs?
- Who else must have input into meeting the needs of our customers, partners, and competitors?

Stakeholders' needs include improved business results, higher return on investment, more effective hiring and retention practices, better organizational communications, improved developmental strategies, and the like. Organizations must identify which of these needs are most prevalent among their stakeholder groups and design strategies to fulfill them.

IDENTIFYING STAKEHOLDER EXPECTATIONS

Identifying expectations is an important way of understanding how employees meet organizational goals. However, all parties need to understand how expectations differ from needs. Expectations are outcomes desired by stakeholders, while needs are requirements that stakeholders must have to maintain satisfactory performance. In other words, needs are the minimal or baseline requirements that must be met for the stakeholder, whether internal or external. Expectations are usually the benchmarks that stakeholders or organizations hope to achieve. Benchmarks (expectations) are higher up the outcome continuum than needs (baselines). Both needs and expectations must be met by stakeholders if organizations are to remain viable.

Expectations are the outcomes that individuals anticipate from an interaction or from an organization's products or services. Expectations should be realistic and attainable because they establish satisfaction levels for stakeholders. That is, expectations are those things that stakeholders assume they will receive as a result of using products or services. Internally, expectations define performance, behavior, and outcomes; they are a means by which performance outcomes are measured and valued.

On the down side, expectations may be set so high as to be unachievable. When this occurs, organizations become melancholy or mediocre as employees fail to see how their work is beneficial or contributory to positive organizational results. Recently, we worked with an organization that believed in setting expectations so high that employees could never reach them. Senior executives felt that this practice motivated their employees. When we asked this group to describe their employees' performance, their response was that they had solid performance results but could not provide measurable examples. Consequently, we had them set achievable, measurable expectations for their employees for the upcoming quarter. Much to their surprise, employees experienced the best performance results of the year. We contributed this to the employees' ability to identify specific, achievable expectations and make adjustments in their performance accordingly.

While visualization of success is important, this activity must be tempered with a realistic perspective of *what* is achievable; setting high, unreachable goals destroys motivation. A workable strategy involves breaking expectations down into small, manageable parts, thus allowing employees to measure success on a smaller scale. Often, when employees cannot visualize success they won't put forth the effort required to obtain satisfactory results.

IDENTIFYING ORGANIZATIONAL REALITIES

Organizations often have a difficult time defining and understanding their realities. Reality is the practical state of an organization at any given time. To understand organizational reality, internal and external forces that drive change within an organization must be accounted for. Reality takes on four different forms: equilibrium, crisis, organizational centeredness, and expansion.

Avoiding Organizational Equilibrium

Organizations in a state of tranquility, balancing business results while meeting stakeholders' needs, are in equilibrium. In this state, organizations are neither leading the pack nor following; instead, they're somewhere in the middle. As a result, these organizations have little opportunity to excel, enjoying a comfort zone that is hard to break free of. While they may meet stakeholder needs, rarely are their expectations exceeded.

Organizations in this state easily lose external customers who are not strongly supportive or enthusiastic about their products or services, but are merely satisfied with deliverables. To overcome this lukewarm condition, organizations must strive to reach each and every standard and benchmark set by stakeholders. If unsuccessful, organizations begin to hemorrhage—they must continuously improve or perish.

Preventing Organizational Crisis

Falling revenue, decreasing market share, declining profits, and dropping stock prices often produce a condition known as organizational crisis. When these problems first surface, senior executives and managers enter a period of shock. They don't know what to do; they appear to be paralyzed. Eventually, this condition is replaced by denial—organizational leaders refuse to accept their present situation. They can't believe it is as bad as it seems. Consequently, leaders fail to search for the real cause of the problem because they are convinced the situation is unreal. Sometimes, organizational leaders attempt to overcome organizational crisis by making dramatic, yet temporary, changes within the organization (i.e., laying off employees, eliminating nonrevenue departments such as human resources or public relations, establishing early retirement plans, etc.) or implementing quick fix solutions to complex problems (i.e., unnecessary training, organizational restructuring, market diversification, etc.). These usually futile attempts to address difficult, complicated problems with simple solutions serve to confuse and compound an already overwhelming situation. If an organization is lucky, its leaders possess the insight, imagination, and determination to address the real problem and its causes.

While adjusting and reacting appropriately to organizational crises is important, preventing them is even more critical. To strategically prevent organizational crises, organizations must focus all of their attention on their most important priority: internal and external stakeholders. In other words, organizations must focus on their stakeholders' needs and expectations by providing them with the products and services they perceive to be of value. Anticipating and articulating stakeholders' needs and expectations allows organizations to:

- embrace rapid, drastic, systematic change required by today's global economy;
- accept changing conditions and demands in the marketplace;
- allocate financial and human resources in appropriate, cost-effective ways;
- develop an early warning system that will prevent them from crashing into corporate icebergs;

- develop and implement strategic corrections necessary to navigate uncharted economic seas.

Overcoming Organizational Centeredness

Some organizations are so confident and comfortable with their positions that they refuse to believe they will ever be caught or surpassed by the competition. These misguided firms are focusing on their own greatness and may eventually "crash and burn." We refer to this as organizational centeredness—which is the equivalence of self-centeredness focused on organizations rather than the individual. Organizations suffering from this phenomenon are punctuated by self-centered senior executives and managers who believe that their current advantages or technological expertise will prevent them from falling into the trap that most commonly occurs for other organizations. Not a single product, service, or organization—with the exception of governmental entities or supported monopolies—can survive long term without experiencing major adjustments. No organization is immune from competition—living in a vacuum creates conditions that eventually lead to downfall. It's not unlike some of the overconfident behavior of military leaders of the failed Roman Empire many centuries ago.

We have seen the rise and fall of organizations again and again. Some organizations suffer delusions of grandeur, believing they have all the answers and the ability to walk on water. IBM and General Electric are two organizations that had to redefine their businesses and respective customers in order to maintain market share and organizational viability. IBM experienced tremendous difficulties in the late 1980s and early 1990s due to feelings of invincibility while General Electric overdiversified; customers were forgotten as they focused upon their own self-interests. Since their periods of organizational hemorrhaging, these companies have made tremendous changes in how they conduct business and are on the road to successfully rebuilding their damaged reputations.

Sears and General Motors, on the other hand, have focused so hard on old-fashioned or outdated approaches to the retail business and product streamlining that they have been unable to successfully defend or recapture market share. While Sears and GM remain viable in terms of sales, revenue, and asset retention, they have been unable to meet the needs and expectations of many stakeholder groups. Both Sears and General Motors remain major players in their respective markets, yet they continue to watch competitors (such as Wal-Mart and Honda) acquire more and more market share with greater success. Both represent classic examples of organizational centeredness from the 1950s, 1960s, 1970s, and 1980s that have produced disappointing results.

Organizationally centered businesses become lazy, believing in their own never-ending superiority and success. They experience a phenomenon known as the *law of fast forgetting*, which refers to how quickly an organization forgets how it became successful. Instead, businesses must focus on changes that will help them maintain and enhance their viability, which can best be done by meeting the needs and expectations of their various stakeholder groups.

Understanding Organizational Expansion

Organizations that set their sights on expansion and integrate that vision with the needs and expectations of their stakeholders are in a prime position to succeed. Having a vision of the future without accounting for stakeholders' needs and expectations is like watching a movie in a foreign language. The viewer has some idea of what is going on because the scenes may be visually interpreted, but because the articulation and rhetoric of what is being communicated are missing, the chance of "getting" the meaning is quite remote.

Organizations that have aligned expansion with internal and external stakeholder needs, expectations, and realities will provide themselves the best opportunities for long-term growth and success. It is critical that organizations understand and examine carefully all stakeholders, defining their roles, responsibilities, needs, and expectations. This inclusive approach to expansion allows organizations to successfully identify and overcome the barriers that prevent their success.

INFORMATION ANALYSIS

One of the best ways of capturing a complete understanding of the needs, expectations, and organizational realities of each stakeholder group is through a comprehensive information analysis activity. Information analysis reveals the needs, expectations, and deficiencies that impact stakeholder behavior and attitudes. An information analysis consists of five steps:

1. Identifying needs/expectations gaps
2. Gathering data

3. Analyzing data
4. Discussing findings with stakeholders
5. Determining appropriate action steps

Prior to embarking on the information analysis process, organizations must challenge their perspectives. By doing so, they are forced to gather data that either support or reject their hypothesis. In this way, organizations document the "evidence" needed to make thoughtful, reasonable recommendations that address stakeholders' unmet needs or unsatisfied expectations.

The information analysis process begins with identifying the needs and expectations (i.e., increased revenue, productivity, improved quality or service) of stakeholders and comparing them to actual outcomes. Stakeholders' needs and expectations are the "desired state," condition, or circumstances preferred, and serve as targets for all operational units, functions, departments, or divisions. The difference between actual outcomes and desired state represents the needs/expectations gap. That is, a needs/expectations gap illustrates the difference between "what is" and "what should be."

Once needs/expectations gaps have been identified, the next step involves examination of data-gathering analysis methods. Relevance and appropriateness of each methodology require scrutiny to ensure selection of the proper mix (Gilley & Maycunich, 1998). A number of strategies may be used to uncover evidence regarding stakeholder groups. The most common methods are:

1. focus groups
2. interviews
3. observations
4. questionnaires

Each of these methods is designed to solicit stakeholders' thoughts and ideas regarding their needs and expectations. Some are more appropriate than others; hence organizations must ascertain under what conditions and circumstances they will utilize various methods. Furthermore, it is better to rely on several sources as opposed to just one. Use of multiple methods allows organizations to be more confident in the data collected, particularly when differing methodologies yield identical results.

At all times, organizations must proceed strategically during the data-gathering process, which includes designing a process that is efficient as well as effective. Organizations must remain objective, guarding against the use of favored analysis methods that may not be appropriate. Biases should be addressed during the first phase of the data-gathering process, which is the identification of assumptions and starting points. Certain assumptions focus information analysis, offering direction as to how information is to be gathered. Once an agreed-on list of analysis methods has been identified, the final step of this process is engaging in the analysis of data.

During the analysis of data phase, organizations examine and interpret the data gathered in step 2 for the purposes of drawing conclusions and identifying implications. Gilley and Maycunich (1998) believe that this seemingly straightforward process presents its own challenges as data are seldom obtained in an absolute, clean, understandable form. They contend that adequately gathering information and selecting analysis methodologies (that garner an optimal amount and type of data necessary to draw conclusions and provide implications) makes data analysis a much simpler process. Once an interpretation has been completed, organizations can prepare the data for presentation to stakeholders.

Discussing findings with stakeholders serves as a reality check, ensures accuracy of data and interpretations, allows buy-in from all parties, and further solidifies the relationship-building process. Presenting findings, conclusions, implications, or recommendations to stakeholders in a formal setting is not recommended as one runs the risk of catching them off guard or sharing information that stakeholders perceive to be confidential. Embarrassing interactions such as these can forever destroy one's credibility with stakeholders. Informal meetings provide a comfortable forum for sharing findings, conclusions, applications, or recommendations that can be held in the strictest confidence or "off the record" (Gilley & Maycunich, 1998). Information that is perceived to be too controversial, politically damaging, or in poor taste should be eliminated from the final presentation. Informal meetings afford stakeholders the opportunity to react before the findings and recommendations become official. They are also an excellent opportunity to integrate the stakeholder insights, perceptions, and suggestions regarding *how* data or recommendations should be presented.

Once findings, conclusions, implications, and recommendations have been thoroughly examined, attention must be turned collectively to formulating action steps. This collaborative activity requires creation of a partnership designed to address the performance challenge. As we will discuss, creating a performance alignment partnership responsible for developing action steps presents the most efficient means of addressing the performance challenge. Then and only then will employees be transformed into the organization's greatest asset.

Action steps can include: implementing the performance alignment process (Chapters 2–8), enhancing leadership effectiveness (Chapter 9), and creating virtual teams (Chapter 10). Each of these helps the organization improve its performance capacity and achieve desired business results. Regardless of the intervention selected, it must help stakeholders meet their needs and satisfy their expectations.

CONCLUSION

The first step in applying the performance alignment model is to conduct stakeholder valuation. By doing so, organizations identify the needs, expectations, and organizational realities of each stakeholder. This information will help improve employee quality and performance, expand market share, and achieve the strategic business goals and objectives of the organization. In addition, organizations will be able to avoid equilibrium, hemorrhaging, centeredness, and expansion practices that prevent them from growing or expanding their business in a positive, effective manner.

By understanding organizational stakeholder needs, expectations, and realities, organizations will be ready to link initiatives with their strategic business goals and objectives. Once this linkage has occurred, enlightened organizations develop job designs that enable employees to perform at the highest possible level—often meeting or exceeding performance standards (see Chapter 3). In this way, organizations link their stakeholders with the performance alignment process.

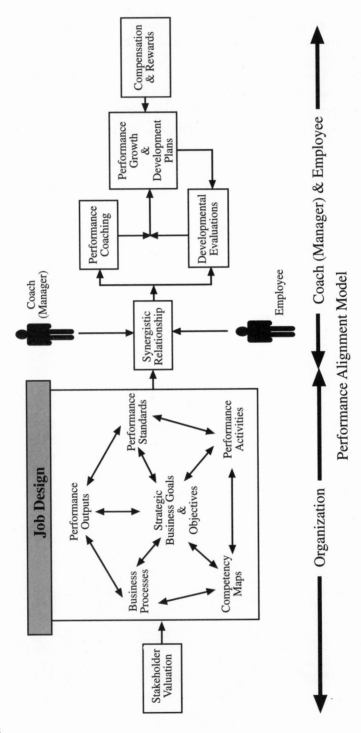

Chapter 3
IMPROVING JOB DESIGN

Once stakeholders' needs and expectations have been identified, organizations can isolate strategies for improving the execution, management, and quality of employee performance. These strategies apply the performance alignment process to the performer (employee) level within the organization. In other words, the same strategy being utilized to address the performance challenge at the organizational level can be used to improve the performance of each employee. Consequently, only one approach need be used to transform employees into the organization's greatest asset.

ORGANIZATIONS AS SYSTEMS

Organizations are systems consisting of various departments, units, and divisions that band together to produce products and services purchased and used by customers and clients—the aggregate of which comprise the marketplace (Figure 3.1). The system approach emphasizes the organization's relationship with its markets and the basic internal functions that comprise any firm (Figure 3.1).

To understand how work is accomplished within organizations, it is necessary to dissect the organizational system into component parts. The first level of an organizational system is the organizational level, consisting of the various departments (functions) that interact with one another in order to produce products and services aimed at the ultimate consumer. The second level of the organizational system is the business process level—the interface between an organizational function (e.g., marketing), business processes (e.g., promotions, market research), and subprocesses (e.g., sales promotions, advertising, personal selling). Finally, the third level of an organizational system is the performer level—where the majority of work is accomplished (Figure 3.1).

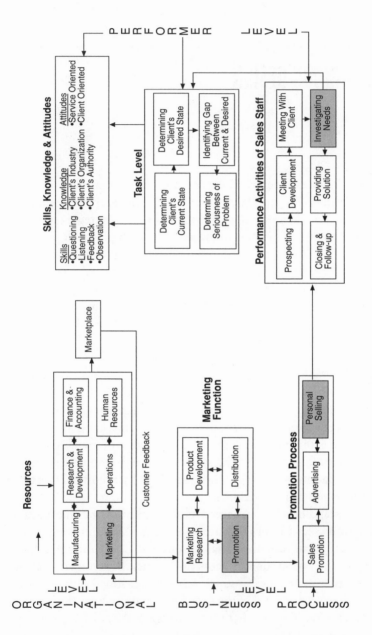

Figure 3.1 Organizational, Business Process, and Performer Levels Combined

38

Breaking down the organizational level into separate functions and business processes reveals an organization's complexity, demonstrating the dependency that separate functions and processes have on one another. This insight reveals how difficult organizational change and performance improvement can be to execute. Analysis such as this does, however, expose leverage points where change initiatives can be most successful.

Each function (department) within an organization consists of subparts arranged to accomplish its work. For example, the marketing function consists of four separate but interrelated parts: promotion, product development, distribution, and marketing research. These components are referred to as *business processes* (Figure 3.1).

While these business processes appear confined within the marketing function, in reality they interact with other business processes housed within other functions. This functional interfacing is necessary to produce internal deliverables that, collectively, comprise the organization's product and service offerings.

Business processes can be further broken down into subprocesses. In the case of the marketing function, the promotion process consists of three parts: sales promotion, advertising, and personal selling (Figure 3.1). It is at this point that job assignments become plentiful. That is, as we descend the organizational pyramid, jobs become more abundant. At the top of the organization fewer jobs exist, the most common of which are senior management, including executive positions. More jobs are housed in organizational functions and even more exist at the business process and subprocess levels.

Identification of subprocesses permits examination of specific performance activities that employees (performers) accomplish. Performance activities are the specific steps employees follow when doing their jobs. Collectively, performance activities define a job. When completed, they result in performance outputs, which are the deliverables an employee is paid to produce. Performance outputs can be internal or external. Internal performance outputs are deliverables used by employees in the successful execution of their jobs, while external performance outputs are delivered directly to an organization's customers.

To examine performance activities, let's return to our example. The personal selling process consists of six performance activities: client prospecting, client development, meeting with clients, investigating client needs, presenting solutions that satisfy client needs, and closing sales and follow-up actions (Figure 3.1). These performance activities collectively constitute a salesperson's job within the organization. Successful implementation of these activities will result in delivery of performance outputs such as effective prospecting, completing an appropriate number of successful sales calls, sales presentations, sales revenue, and the like.

Each performance activity consists of a number of individual tasks required for its completion. For example, four separate tasks are required when investigating client needs: (1) determining the client's current situation, (2) determining the client's desired situation, (3) investigating the gap between the current and desired situation in quantifiable and qualifiable terms expressed as a problem or need, and (4) evaluating the seriousness of the client's problem or need (Figure 3.1).

Finally, employees must have specific knowledge, skills, and attitudes to successfully complete each task within their job classification. For example, salespeople must possess knowledge of their clients' organization and industry, a service-oriented attitude, and questioning, listening, observation, and feedback skills to be successful in uncovering client needs (Figure 3.1).

Combination of the organization, business process, and performer levels creates the total organizational system. Each level consists of critical components working in harmony to produce the desired performance outputs to be delivered to internal or external stakeholders (see Chapter 2). Opportunities for improved effectiveness and efficiency lie in the quality of performance at all levels within the organization. An organizational or performance breakdown requires determination of breakdown location (at which level did the breakdown occur?), and its impact on the two other levels.

According to Rummler and Brache (1995), "the greatest opportunity for performance improvement often lies in functional interface—those points at which the baton . . . is being passed from one department (function) to another" (p. 9). Key interfaces might include: product ideas being handed off from the marketing research and development department (business process) to the manufacturing department; a compensation plan created by the human resource department being handed to operations for administration; or an insurance claim being transferred from the claims area to accounting for payment. The greatest opportunity for breakdown also occurs during these exchanges. Improving interdepartmental interfacing provides an organization with opportunities to enhance the ultimate delivery of products and services to its customers.

GOALS, DESIGN, AND MANAGEMENT

According to Rummler and Brache (1995), each of the three levels of an organizational system differs in its goals, design, and management, which are the factors determining effectiveness. Goals represent the specific outcomes that reflect an organization's department, business process, and performer (employee) performance expectations as well as internal or external stakeholders' needs and expectations. Design refers to how each level is organized to achieve its respective goals. Management involves the practices employed to ensure that goals are achieved.

Organizational Level

At the organizational level, the firm's principal aim is its strategic business goals and objectives. Strategic business goals and objectives include total revenue expectations, revenue increases over the previous term (expressed in percentages), net operating income, competitive position, product development, percentage of profitability increases, resource utilization, quality specifications, desired market penetration, stockholder dividend requirements, and so on.

The type of blueprint needed at the organizational level is commonly referred to as organizational design, which includes organizational structure, culture, and work climate. Through organizational design, departmental boundaries and reporting relationships are clearly established.

Organizational management entails practices used to guarantee that internal functions achieve their respective goals. The most important type of management practice is performance management, which the performance alignment process was designed to improve. That is, the performance alignment process was created to help organizations manage performance at the macro (organizational) level. In this way, organizations manage human and material resources, improve interfaces between functions and business processes, and enhance performance outputs generated by employees (performers). The performance alignment process simultaneously improves each of these three components.

Business Process Level

Business processes are the vehicles through which work is produced; thus, organizations must set goals for each of their processes (Rummler

& Brache, 1995). Process goals are established by each function (department or business unit) within the organization. These goals collectively exist to help the organization meet the needs and expectations of its internal and external stakeholders.

Once process goals are established, business processes should be designed to maximize performance outputs. Formal structures are important to the accentuation of performance outputs, while job design should exemplify best practices. The overall impact on organizational effectiveness is decidedly positive.

The management of business process levels should focus on the same ingredients as organizational management, including goal, performance, resource, and interface management (Rummler & Brache, 1995). In short, management of business processes is identical to organizational management except that it occurs on a smaller, more manageable scale.

Performer Level

Organizational interface with internal and external stakeholders occurs at the performer level—where employees actually do the work required to produce products and services. The organizational and business process levels may be architectural masterpieces, but if performers cannot execute efficiently and effectively, performance quality and outputs will be negatively affected. Unless organizations create conditions by which their employees can produce adequate products and services, organizational process goals will be jeopardized. Thus, the performer level is critical to the ultimate success of any organization and must be managed accordingly.

Performer goals Performer goals are established for each employee in order to support business processes and organizational objectives. These goals should be established during the developmental evaluation process (see Chapter 6) and become the focus of growth and development plans (see Chapter 7).

Performer goals encompass a variety of targeted activities. They can be written exclusively to improve individual performance or quality, or in such a way as to improve employee growth and development. Performer goals are the backbone of the performance alignment process, serving as the individual targets employees shoot for on a daily basis. They should be written with the organization's strategic business goals and objectives in mind; thus, performer goals are linked to business strategy. Performer goals can include:

- acquisition of new job skills intended to improve performance outputs and activities
- acquisition of new knowledge that will help employees with complex problem-solving or decision-making activities on the job
- acquisition or improvement of attitudes associated with one's performance activities
- targeted performance improvement activities (i.e., increase in sales volume, number of claims processed, amount of sales calls made, number of customer service interventions completed, etc).
- improvement in quality or production
- improvement in timeliness of delivery

Job design Job design is the fundamental design activity that maximizes performance (Figure 3.2). Job design consists of six separate but interrelated components. At the heart of job design are the organization's strategic business goals and objectives, which focus performers' activities. Jobs that do not help an organization achieve its strategic business goals and objectives cease to be valuable. It is extremely important, therefore, to link all job design activities to these goals and objectives.

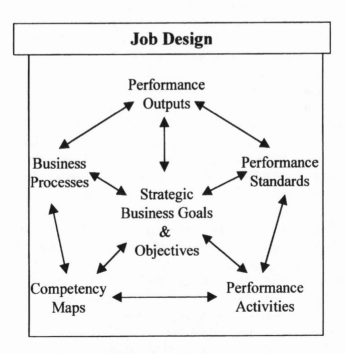

Figure 3.2 Job Design

Each job within an organization is housed within a business process. As previously discussed, a business process is a subpart of an organizational function. An organizational function is commonly referred to as departments or business units within organizations. Job design examines the smallest components of the chain. Therefore, breakdowns or improvements in the interface between business processes will ultimately impact organizational performance capacity. Thus, job design activities should uncover opportunities for performance improvement. Once business process interfaces have been identified, four interrelated components require examination: performance outputs, performance activities, performance standards, and competency maps.

Performance outputs are the deliverables that employees are paid to produce. Deliverables can be generated for both internal and external usage. Internally focused performance outputs consist of deliverables used by other employees in the execution of their jobs, typically when producing deliverables intended for the marketplace. External deliverables are those products or services made available to customers outside the organization.

Performance activities are the steps in which employees engage in the creation of performance outputs. As stated previously, they are the small steps employees take to complete a job. Each performance activity consists of micro tasks, which collectively form the steps in an employee's job. For example, our salesperson's job entails six performance activities. When used in combination, these activities generate the above performance deliverables.

Performance standards are the targets used to measure the quality of employee performance outputs and the efficiency of their performance activities. Performance standards represent two distinctly different measurement criteria. Those standards used for performance outputs identify the excellence criteria used in measuring quality of products and services. In contrast, performance standards linked to performance activities identify best practices. Nevertheless, performance standards serve as targets for employees when generating performance outputs or executing performance activities, and are extremely important when improving both performance effectiveness and efficiency. Without performance standards, employees will have no idea whether they are creating performance outputs or executing performance activities acceptable to internal or external stakeholders.

The last component of the job design framework is *competency maps*, which consist of the knowledge, skills, and attitudes an employee must have to complete job tasks that comprise performance activities. Competency maps can be quite complex as they reflect all the knowledge, skills, and appropriate attitudes employees must possess to adequately complete performance activities used in generating performance outputs.

Competency maps are useful in recruiting and selection of employees for a given job classification. They can also be used to determine the training and development activities in which employees must participate to acquire adequate levels of performance mastery. In short, competency maps are an evaluation tool useful in determining employee strengths and weaknesses, thereby serving as a template in formulating performance growth and development plans.

Performer management While the performance alignment process was designed to help organizations address the performance challenge, it can also be used to help manage each employee's performance. That is, the performance alignment process is appropriate for and can be applied to the performer level.

The performance alignment process evolves from an organizational performance strategy to a performance management application, useful with each and every employee regardless of level or job responsibilities. This application requires no additional components or steps, but does necessitate a minor modification in the performance alignment process model—a modification that is more a realignment of steps than a new application or undertaking. The best way of demonstrating the performance alignment process' application to the performer level involves: (1) examining the traditional performance process and the performance management processes utilized by so many organizations, (2) identifying faulty assumptions and shortcomings of these approaches, (3) applying the various components of the performance alignment process to the performer level, and (4) evaluating improvements in results. Doing so clarifies how each additional component enriches the performance management process.

Applying the Performance Alignment Process to the Performer Level

Many organizations employ a performance process that consists of five simple steps (Figure 3.3). The process begins by identifying and assembling the material resources required to produce specific deliverables (performance outputs). Material resources can include raw materials, component parts, information, product specification sheets and diagrams, tools, equipment, computers, telephones, fax machines, or any other resources required for job completion. Next, the performer (employee)

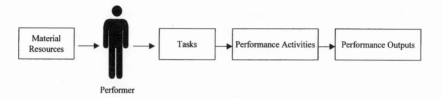

Figure 3.3 Traditional Performance Process

is responsible for generating specific performance deliverables, for which he or she must possess the appropriate knowledge, skills, and attitudes to be successful.

If knowledge, skill, and attitude levels are appropriate, performers are able to execute the separate steps required to produce a deliverable. Each step is referred to as a task, the combination of which comprise performance activities. A performance deliverable is produced when performers put into action each of the above four steps. In other words, performers transform material resources into performance outputs by following a series of predetermined tasks, which collectively constitute performance activities.

This common approach often produces acceptable results, yet the traditional performance process allows for several omissions that lead to poor performance quality or inadequate productivity. The most notable omission is the lack of performance standards used to evaluate the quality of performance activities and outputs. Other omissions are the absence of performance feedback necessary to ensure timely, quality deliverables and the lack of performance appraisal and compensation reward reviews that guarantee long-term performance improvement.

A principal assumption made by users of the traditional approach is that employees possess the knowledge, skills, and attitudes necessary to adequately perform tasks. Another erroneous assumption is the belief that performers are properly trained to execute each task correctly and in the proper sequence (performance activities). The traditional approach is also based on the belief that employees are self-sufficient, requiring little or no performance feedback or evaluation.

In essence, the traditional performance process approach is easy to execute, requiring little more than an appropriate quantity of material resources, a performer, and a job designed at a minimal level of correctness. While this approach *can* help organizations produce products and services that enable them to remain competitive and profitable, numerous important steps are omitted and assumptions made that negatively impact performance quality and quantity.

Most organizations realize that the traditional performance process has several limitations; consequently, they use a modified version designed to overcome its shortfalls (Figure 3.4). We refer to this approach as the performance management process since an element of quality control has been added to ensure performance quality and quantity. This approach can be differentiated from the traditional performance approach in three distinct ways. First, performance standards are developed and applied that help performers produce outputs and execute activities at the highest possible levels of quality. Performance standards also help employees monitor performance activities and evaluate their deliverables. Second, performance feedback and reinforcement ensure that performers receive specific, timely, substantive information regarding their work and output production. Feedback and reinforcement are commonly delivered to performers by managers and supervisors, intended to help employees correct or improve their performance. Third, the performance management process utilizes modified performance appraisals and compensation and reward reviews to provide employees with *formal feedback* regarding their efforts, and to communicate compensation and rewards for their performance. Historically, such reviews are conducted on an annual basis, consisting of simple performance appraisal forms and one-on-one discussions with managers or supervisors. The quality of performance reviews varies from organization to organization and can be as simple as a five-minute performance appraisal interview or as complicated as a 360-degree evaluation process.

In Figure 3.4 we illustrate performance standards, performance appraisal, and reinforcement and feedback processes with dotted lines to emphasize the infrequent, disoriented nature of such activities. During this phase of performance management, organizations often approach these activities as necessary evils that must be applied or used. As a result, managers and supervisors approach them reluctantly, failing to capture the enormous benefits such activities can yield. In addition, performance appraisal activities are typically conducted to determine the correctness of performance rather than as a means of enhancing employee relationships or performance growth and development.

Other shortcomings of the performance management process include failing to engage employees in performance growth and development planning useful in enhancing performance capacity. This planning is the natural outgrowth of the performance alignment process. Managers' and supervisors' reluctance at this point prohibits them

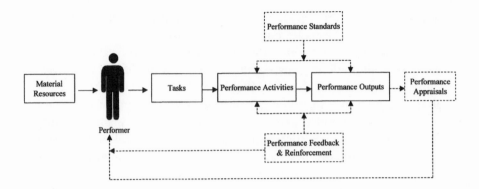

Figure 3.4 Traditional Performance Management Process

from spending valuable time with employees engaged in the design of learning acquisition and transfer activities that foster growth and development. Another shortfall is the lack of formal performance coaching activities useful in training employees, positively confronting performance, or providing counseling and mentoring opportunities designed to further develop employees' capabilities. Finally, organizations that use the performance management process seldom separate compensation and reward reviews from performance appraisals. Because of this orientation, compensation and reward strategies fail to link performance growth and development activities with organizational initiatives, further preventing employees from perceiving performance appraisals as anything but necessary evils. When these two activities are separated into distinctly different actions, employees approach performance appraisals as developmental opportunities, and compensation and reward reviews as ways of determining the amount and type of formal reinforcement necessary to encourage continuous performance growth or development.

Figure 3.5 illustrates the performance alignment process' bearing on the performer level. Close examination of this diagram reveals each of the performance alignment component's application to the individual performer—the organization's most micro level. When the process is applied to the performer level, performance standards are in place for employees to gauge the quality of their deliverables and activities. At this point, developmental evaluations replace the traditional performance appraisal process, encouraging performance growth and development as well as utilization of learning acquisition and transfer plans. Additionally, informal, sporadic performance feedback or reinforcement is

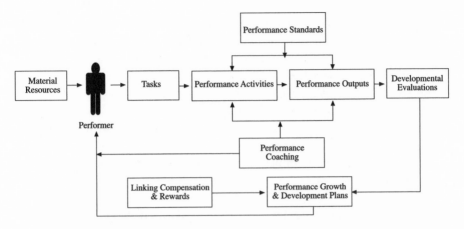

Figure 3.5 Performance Alignment Applied to the Performer Level

replaced by formalized performance coaching activities that train, confront, counsel, and mentor employees. Finally, compensation and rewards are directly linked to performance growth and development planning activities to remunerate employees for ever-increasing knowledge, skills, and attitudes applied to the job.

We are assuming that stakeholder valuations have been conducted in order to apply the performance alignment process at the organizational level. Therefore, duplication of this activity at the performer level is unnecessary. Any job assignments applied to the performance alignment process at the performer level should account for identified stakeholder needs and expectations, thus becoming permanent components of performance standards and the developmental evaluation process used to assess employee performance.

Our final assumption is that all job assignments are directly linked to the organization's strategic business goals and objectives and, therefore, the application of the performance alignment process at the performer level incorporates such an understanding. In this way, performers' jobs are forever linked to the organization's business strategy, guaranteeing direct, positive impact on the organization's results.

CONCLUSION

Organizations are systems consisting of three distinct levels: organizational, business process, and performer. Each level requires evaluation based on its goals, design, and management practices. While often more expedient to view organizational management from a macro level, the performance challenge can be best addressed by applying the concepts, principles, and ideas of the performance alignment process model at both the organizational and performer levels. It is important to note that the components, ideas, and principles embedded in the performance alignment process can indeed help manage individual employees at the performer level. In this way, one organization-wide strategy of addressing the performance challenge may be applied.

The performance alignment process model (Job Design section) can be used when:

- employees focus on less important activities (reason 1)
- there are barriers or obstacles preventing adequate performance (reason 2)
- employees' jobs are poorly designed (reason 3)
- employees don't know how to measure or evaluate their performance (reason 4, see Figure 1.3)

The performance alignment process model (Job Design) helps an organization link performance to its strategic business goals and objectives (reason 2) and identify performance breakdowns (reason 3, Figure 1.2).

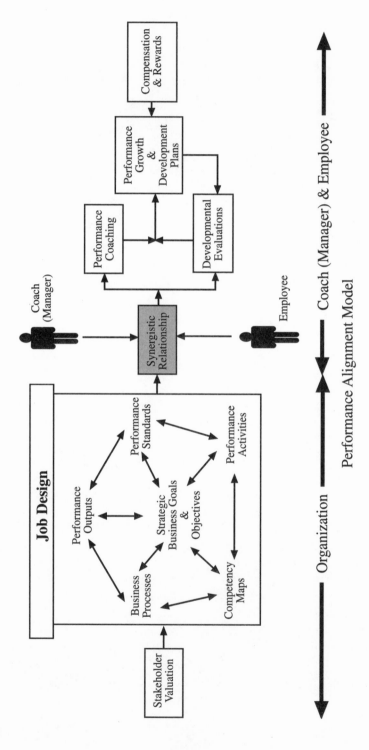

Performance Alignment Model

Chapter 4

ESTABLISHING SYNERGISTIC RELATIONSHIPS

Organizations spend large sums of money recruiting and hiring managers whose pedigrees look good on paper. Organizations do this because they blindly believe that an individual's pedigree is the most important hiring criterion—more essential than his or her ability to work with people. Consequently, people are hired for their technical knowledge, expertise, or educational degrees from the most prestigious business schools rather than for their "managerial skills." By hiring this way, organizations discount the importance of interpersonal skills necessary to achievement of desired business results. Ultimately, employees are unmotivated, unproductive, uncooperative, and unhappy.

In the first chapter, we discussed why organizations fail and illustrated how important it is for organizations to understand that all employees have needs that must be satisfied in the workplace. Daniel Goleman, in his revolutionary book, *Emotional Intelligence*, adds that managers must understand the importance of managing the whole person rather than individual attributes such as knowledge, IQ, or expertise. Thus, organizations must fulfill the work-related emotional needs of each employee. When this occurs, we will see a dramatic shift in how organizations operate.

All people, whether inside an organization or in their personal lives, must have one basic need met—the "ability to love oneself," commonly called self-esteem. This occurs in our personal lives via interactions with loved ones and friends. In the workplace, this need is met through interactions with co-workers, managers, and organizational leaders. Unfortunately, this basic need is rarely met. All too often, organizations treat employees with little respect, yet demand that they deliver on everything that is asked. Why can't organizations understand that basic needs must be met to achieve organizational harmony and efficiency (see Chapter 10)?

The only way to achieve organizational harmony is for managers to improve their interpersonal skills so that employees feel good about their contributions and accomplishments. By doing so, organizations will be empathetic entities, focusing their energies on building relationships and fulfilling the developmental needs of every employee. Goleman stated, "a key social ability is empathy, understanding others' feelings and taking their perspectives, and respecting the differences in how people feel about things. Relationships are a major focus, including learning to be good listeners and questioners; distinguishing between what someone says or does and your own reaction and judgments; being assertive rather than aggressive or passive; and learning the art of cooperation, conflict resolution, and negotiating compromise" (p. 268). Many of these ideas are embedded in and addressed throughout this book. One of the most critical components is building *synergistic relationships.*

SYNERGISTIC RELATIONSHIPS

Synergy can be defined as the interaction between individuals whose combined efforts are more impactful than if they were to work alone. Synergistic relationships, therefore, are the interdependence of individuals working toward a common goal, which simultaneously provides for growth and development opportunities for both participants as well as the organization.

According to Gilley and Boughton (1996), synergistic relationships are healthy relationships between managers (performance coaches) and their employees, which yield five benefits:

1. Enhancing and building managers' and employees' self-esteem.
2. Enhancing productivity.
3. Enhancing and building organizational communications.
4. Enhancing and building organizational understanding.
5. Enhancing and building organizational commitment (p. 72).

To better understand synergistic relationships complete the following exercise. Take a piece of paper and draw two columns. The header for one column is "characteristics of healthy working relationships," and the other, "characteristics of unhealthy working relationships." In each column, list what you perceive to be indicative of each type of relationship. Most of what exists in healthy relationships can be found in your personal life, while unhealthy characteristics are common in the workplace.

What elements produce healthy personal relationships, and why can't they be at the center of all organizational interactions? The most commonly identified reason is that personal relationships involve freedom to participate. In other words, you have a choice. Is this always the case? What about your family? Most positive, healthy relationships, including those with family members, are the result of free will. In organizations, employees are "stuck" working with certain types of people that make it difficult to produce positive synergy. Nevertheless, some working relationships are better than personal ones. In order to foster positive, healthy working relationships, managers need to understand how to build, grow, and improve them. In short, organizations must develop an approach that can be used to build positive, healthy, and synergistic relationships.

We believe that creating synergistic relationships will help employees who:

- don't feel safe asking for help (reason 5)
- are fearful of repercussions for doing their jobs incorrectly (reason 6)
- don't trust their managers (reason 7, see Figure 1.3)

This process also helps organizations overcome managerial malpractice (reason 4, see Figure 1.2).

Gilley and Boughton (1996) identified a nine-step process for building positive, healthy, and synergistic relationships. The steps are: freedom from fear, communication, interaction, acceptance, personal involvement, trust, honesty, self-esteeming, and professional development (Figure 4.1).

Freedom from Fear

Fear damages lives, hurts relationships, and stifles growth. Fear is one of the primary reasons that employees do not successfully complete their assignments. Moreover, fear of the unknown or of possible repercussions destroys employee morale, confidence, or entrepreneurial spirit. To eliminate fear and improve effectiveness and profitability, organizations must prevent managers from mistreating employees when they do not perform adequately or do not achieve the organizational results needed. Managers must stop treating employees with a lack of respect and with a cavalier, dismissive attitude.

Can fear be healthy? Of course—healthy fear stimulates positive

Figure 4.1 Synergistic Relationship Model
Adapted from Gilley, Jerry W., and Boughton, Nathaniel W., *Stop Managing, Start Coaching!*, McGraw-Hill, 1996, New York.

action in employees. It drives and challenges employees to take responsibility for what they do. For example, a salesperson may have a fear of making cold calls on potential clients while realizing that he or she will not be successful unless he or she makes the calls. This realization helps the salesperson overcome the fear of meeting with clients. The critical difference with this type of fear is that employees do not feel that they are going to be belittled, embarrassed, or humiliated for their efforts. Instead, they feel a sense of accomplishment, hope, and positive reinforcement for a job well done.

Organizations must take the time to create environments that are devoid of negative or retributional fear. Such environments can be developed if employees are allowed to take risks without fear of reprisal and if managers support their employees' efforts and contributions. Unfortunately, too many organizations punish employees for "thinking outside the box" or for behaving differently from the norm. In fact, organizations with homogeneous populations that operate like robots are less effective in addressing performance problems than are ones whose employees are encouraged to foster and demonstrate creativity, independence, and diversity (Gilley & Maycunich, 1998).

To create work environments free of fear, organizations must break down the wall of autocratic persecution and hire managers who will champion employee performance growth and development. Organizations must consider the benefits that can be derived from unleashing the collective minds of their employees, and compare them to the cost of relinquishing power and authority to the individuals who do the work. In other words, encouraging risk taking, creativity, and ownership of problems and their solutions allows employees the opportunities to grow and develop, which could result in a windfall of productivity, profitability, and revenue enhancement. Organizations may also be surprised at the effects such encouragement will have on employee morale, attitudes, and commitment.

Communication

Once an organization has created a positive work environment free of fear, the next step is to improve communications between managers and employees—regardless of their organizational level. Improving communications requires managers to shift their managerial style from authoritarian to participatory (Gilley & Eggland, 1992). This can be done by relinquishing control and dominance over employees, allowing them to participate as equal partners. This transformation requires managers to recognize and accept that their employees have a great deal of experiences, insight, and expertise that should be acknowledged, tapped, and applied. Finally, in order to demonstrate the value and importance of employees' ideas and thoughts, managers must become active participants during communication instead of passive receivers.

Once managers have established a participatory communications style, they should further develop their own interpersonal skills. These skills help managers gather important information from employees, gain further understanding of their employees' points of view, encourage employees to share their feelings, and provide moments of silence that can help employees reflect and reconsider their ideas, thoughts, and positions. These skills serve as a road map, helping managers maneuver and adjust to the ebbs and flows of communication during exchanges with employees.

Relationship skills To improve interpersonal communication, managers should focus on relationship skills that consist of the following:

- Attentiveness
- Empathy
- Genuineness
- Nonverbal techniques
- Rapport
- Understanding

Relationship skills allow managers to enhance their relationships with employees. They help managers build a positive, comfortable, and non-threatening communication climate with employees—one that encourages employees to discuss performance problems, career alternatives and options, and organizational development ideas openly and honestly, without fear of reprisal (Gilley & Boughton, 1996). Such an environment establishes conditions that will expedite the synergistic relationship process.

Attentiveness Attentiveness is the effort made by a manager to hear the message conveyed by an employee. When demonstrated appropriately, employees feel that managers are interested in their problems, points of view, thoughts, and ideas. Attentiveness requires active listening skills and the ability to resist interrupting employees when they are speaking.

Empathy When managers demonstrate the ability to understand their employees' vantage points, they are practicing empathy. Managers who are able to describe the thoughts and feelings of their employees are also demonstrating empathic behavior. Gilley and Eggland (1992) believe that empathetic understanding is the manager's ability to recognize, sense, and understand the feelings that employees communicate through their behavioral and verbal expressions, and to accurately communicate this understanding to employees.

Genuineness Genuineness refers to managers' ability to be themselves in all work situations rather than playing a part or role. Genuineness occurs when managers know who they are and what is important to them, and act on this knowledge accordingly. Moreover, genuineness implies being honest and candid with employees while serving as a manager. Sometimes this requires self-disclosure, but does not necessitate a total unveiling of one's personal or professional life.

Nonverbal techniques One of the best ways of demonstrating an interest in and acceptance of employees is to use nonverbal techniques. These are also important to establishing a positive communications climate. Effective eye contact, nods of the head, and forward engaging body language are the most common types of body language.

Rapport Unconditional positive regard between managers and employees is the result of rapport. Rapport is more than a superficial relationship; it is a deep concern for the well-being of employees. It is demonstrated when managers are as interested in their employees as they are the results they produce. Rapport is established through a manager's sincere interest in, and acceptance of, employees (Gilley & Boughton, 1996).

Understanding Recognizing and correctly interpreting the feelings, thoughts, and behavior of employees is referred to as understanding. While it is impossible to completely understand employees, understanding is essentially the process of sharing experiences, perspectives, and personal and professional histories. Understanding can take two forms, internal and external. Internal understanding is the ability of managers to step into the perceptual world of their employees, including their fears, successes, and failures. External understanding is managers' awareness of their employees' actions and behaviors.

Interaction

To successfully build synergistic relationships, everyone throughout an organization needs to interact on a regular basis. Interaction is more than communication because it implies a personal engagement with employees. Managers and executives must take the time to discuss issues and problems with employees. They must also take time getting to know employees as people. This requires face-to-face interaction.

Unfortunately, many executives and managers spend very little time interacting with employees. Yet, research has clearly demonstrated that employee satisfaction can be greatly enhanced through collaborative interaction with managers and organizational leaders (Gilley & Maycunich, 1998; Bolton, 1986).

Managers must spend time listening, learning, and interacting with each employee in order to build positive synergistic relationships. In fact, spending time with employees helps managers build credibility. The following example demonstrates this point. Recently a senior executive was having difficult interacting with his employees. We discovered that he was primarily communicating with his employees through e-mail and voice mail. We recommended that he walk through his department several times a day and initiate conversations with his employees—which he began doing immediately. During the next few months, his department improved its performance output and financial numbers significantly. The senior executive believes that it was directly related to spending "real, personal time" with people. While this may appear to be an overly simple solution to a complex performance problem, it does work.

Increased contact time (interaction quantity) with employees is just the beginning. Interaction quality remains equally important. To improve a manager's quality of interaction, several techniques—referred to as *following skills*—prove helpful.

Following skills Managers must use skills that help them understand the thoughts and ideas of their employees. In order to accomplish this, managers must allow employees to do most of the talking. We believe that four skills help managers better follow their employees during one-on-one conversations: active listening, encouraging, questioning, and silence.

Active listening One of the most important skills that managers can develop is active listening. Managers spend as much as 70 percent of their waking hours communicating, with over half that time involved in listening. Improving one's listening skills helps reduce disagreements with employees, improves data gathering, and enhances understanding of employees' points of view.

In order to develop better listening skills, managers should:

1. Concentrate all their physical and mental energy on listening
2. Avoid interrupting the speaker
3. Demonstrate interest and alertness
4. Seek an area of agreement with the employee
5. Demonstrate patience
6. Search for meaning and avoid getting hung up on specific words
7. Provide clear and unambiguous feedback to the employee
8. Repress the tendency to respond emotionally to what is said
9. Ask questions when they do not understand something
10. Withhold evaluation of the message until the employee is finished and understanding of the message is mutual (Gilley & Eggland, 1992)

Encouraging Encouraging is a technique that allows employees to expand or elaborate about how they feel. Encouraging sends a message to employees that what they are saying is important and they should continue until they are comfortable with another understanding. Common encouraging techniques include: "I understand," "tell me more," "how so?", "I hear you," nods of the head, and so on. These serve to strengthen employees' responses and their efforts to continue speaking.

Questioning One of the most effective yet sometimes overused following techniques is questioning. If used too often, employees will feel as though they are being interrogated. Asking questions is a critical technique for improving understanding and gathering data but should be used carefully in order to avoid abuse. Questioning is an excellent way of guiding and directing the conversation with employees and helps create structure during an interaction. The most common type of questions are open-ended and closed-ended. Open-ended questions generally require more than a few words to answer and allow employees to expand the conversation in several different directions. In contrast, closed-ended questions can be answered specifically, in relatively few words.

Silence Silence is a very difficult following technique for most managers to master because it can make managers and employees uncomfortable during an interaction. When appropriately used, silence helps employees think through what has transpired and provide additional information or explanations. With practice, managers can use silence in combination with other following techniques, such as active listening and encouraging, to allow employees the opportunity to freely express themselves. Overuse of silence communicates lack of interest on the part of managers and, therefore, should be used as a way of encouraging employee involvement.

Communication killer: technology The development of advanced technology has encouraged organizations to use voice mail and e-mail to distribute greater and greater amounts of information to more and more people. Unfortunately, these techniques encourage more one-way memos and other types of "junk-mail" correspondence that do not improve organizational communications.

Repeatedly, we have seen employees, managers, and executives sending e-mail correspondence to fellow workers instead of engaging in one-on-one personal conversations. Such a strategy eliminates opportunities for two-way interactions and improved understanding. A more serious problem is advanced technology's failure to allow reactions to what is being said or to interpret subtle messages.

Due to the global nature of business, we concede that organizations need to use these technologies to communicate messages. Nevertheless, we recommend that voice mail and e-mail be limited to those messages that have little or no potential for being misunderstood or those that are informative in nature. This ensures that complex messages use approaches that employ face-to-face communications.

Acceptance

As managers interact with their employees, they discover that each is an individual with unique characteristics, personality, life experiences, and professional paths. Based on such a myriad of factors, employees are as different as snowflakes, requiring managers to accept each employee's uniqueness rather than look for similarities.

Consequently, managers must spend time getting to know their employees and discovering how their personalities differ. Managers must guard against the bias that all people are the same and should be treated the same. Managers must understand that strength lies in individual differences and that it is their responsibility to challenge employees to capitalize on their unique gifts.

Acceptance requires respect for employees as persons or worth. In Carl Rogers' (1961) classic work *On Becoming a Person*, he stated, "by acceptance I mean a warm regard for him/her as a person of unconditional self worth . . . an acceptance of and a regard for his/her attitudes, behaviors, and thoughts no matter how negative or positive" (p. 79).

Personal Involvement

Acceptance is a prerequisite to personal involvement, which requires managers to spend significant time with each of their employees. Without this involvement, managers will never be able to develop the type of synergy that improves organizational performance and quality.

Personal involvement does not mean that managers overstep the personal boundaries established by the organization, but instead requires engaging in conversations that enable managers and employees to create a personal bond. Self-disclosure requires managers to open up, sharing both personal and professional information and revealing to employees that they are real human beings with feelings and emotions—in short, demonstrating that they are real people. Second, managers can create personal involvement through observation. Any work station provides clues as to what is important to an employee. This could include pictures of spouses, children, pets, or outdoor activities with friends, awards, books, objects of affection, and so on. Regardless, managers can discover a wealth of information with little effort.

Another type of observation, *relationship analysis*, helps managers discover a great deal about employees' social patterns and relationships. Relationship analysis identifies an employee's socialization pattern and how this pattern is used in the workplace. The purpose of relationship analysis is to simply identify the pattern to promote better understanding of an employee. Regardless of what is discovered, managers should not judge or evaluate the social pattern—they should simply observe and attempt to understand it.

Conducting relationship analysis involves simply watching and observing employees interact with other employees on a daily basis. These interactions reveal a great deal about employees' values and beliefs because people seldom spend time with those they feel uncomfortable with.

The primary benefits of relationship analysis include helping managers discover who employees feel comfortable with and who they may desire to work with on future job assignments. It also helps managers identify with their employees by pointing out mutual colleagues and friends.

Third, managers can improve personal involvement by asking questions that help them discover unique and interesting things about their employees. Managers should take every opportunity to discover important events that occur in their employees' lives as well as uncover the things that hold personal meaning to them. Most people like talking about themselves so let them. Employees like it when others take a personal interest in them as human beings instead of as employees.

Trust

One of the most common problems in today's organizations is the lack of trust between managers and their employees. Why is this the case? It is our belief that trust does not exist because managers fail to:

- establish work environments free of fear
- communicate with employees
- interact with employees on an ongoing basis
- accept employees as unique human beings
- become personally involved with their employees

Establishing trust is hard work. When trust is earned, it is because managers have established a working relationship free of fear, listened attentively and communicated with employees, engaged in conversations that encourage interaction, accepted employees as unique individuals, and taken the opportunity to become personally involved with employees. In other words, trust is granted because a manager has successfully accomplished each of the five previous steps of the synergistic relationship model.

In working relationships trust is earned, not granted because of someone's pedigree or title. Because managers have power or authority over employees, it does not guarantee that employees will trust them. Trust is based on truth, which implies open, honest, and direct communication. Consequently, hidden agendas are avoided and discouraged, while employees and managers are encouraged to be forthright.

Several *"trust killers"* prevent managers from gaining employees' loyalty and acceptance. They include:

- Criticizing—making unwarranted negative comments about employees' performance, attitudes, and decisions.
- Diagnosing—playing amateur psychiatrist by analyzing employees' motives and behaviors.
- Advising—giving employees "the solution" to their problems without asking for their input.
- Ordering—coercing and forcing employees to do things management's way.
- Threatening—controlling employees' actions with intimidating, negative consequences.
- Avoiding—resisting logical or reasonable requests because managers disagree with employees or simply want to be difficult.
- Questioning—the "Sergeant Friday routine," questioning every decision, idea, recommendation, or suggestion (Gilley & Boughton, 1996).

Honesty

Does honesty come before or after trust? When building synergistic relationships, we have found that trust leads to honesty. As managers establish trust, employees begin sharing more and more information with them and the level of professional intimacy increases. Allow us to apply this philosophy to the executive we discussed earlier. As he became more interactive with his employees, he discovered that they reciprocated in a personal, positive manner. He found that having personal conversations with his employees about their interests, families, and friends caused them to become engaging and responsive. Over time, his employees began to trust him. Much to his surprise they began to talk to him about issues facing the organization. Once he established trust, honesty followed in the form of straightforward conversations regarding the way the organization could improve its productivity and quality—information that is critical in making better and more informed decisions and important when implementing change interventions in an organization. By leaving the ivory tower, our executive friend was able to establish a deeper level of professional intimacy, which helped improve relationships and results.

Assertive communication When working with employees managers will have to confront their performance (see Chapter 5). How can this be done while still maintaining a positive working relationship? It certainly cannot be accomplished through aggressive, rude, abusive, or sarcastic tactics by which managers dominate employees and attempt to force changes in behavior. These methods only create resentment and seldom help resolve performance problems. Working relationships cannot be achieved by avoiding problems and pretending they do not exist. While a submissive approach does not produce a direct confrontation, which can cause resentment and anger, it only postpones dealing with performance problems at a later date. Eventually problems must be addressed—typically when performance has deteriorated to such a point that drastic action must be taken. Often such action makes the situation even worse.

The only way managers can confront employees' performance problems and still maintain positive work relationships is through assertive communication. Assertive communication involves nonjudgmental descriptions of the performance behaviors requiring change. It allows managers to disclose their feelings about an employee behavior without affixing blame. Assertive communication clarifies the effects of employee behavior on managers and the organization. In other words, assertive communication is a straightforward communication technique designed to confront performance problems in a nonthreatening, factual, and direct manner so that employees understand what they are doing wrong and its impact on the organization.

Assertive communication enables managers to maintain employees' self-respect, personal happiness, confidence, and satisfaction. This type of communication allows managers to stand up for their own rights and express their personal needs, values, concerns, and ideas in direct and appropriate ways. While meeting their own needs, managers don't violate the needs of their employees while simultaneously helping employees retain a positive self-concept. According to Gilley and Boughton (1996), true assertiveness is a way of behaving that confirms the manager's own individual worth and dignity while simultaneously confirming and maintaining the worth and dignity of employees.

Self-Esteeming

Self-esteeming can be defined as mutual and reciprocal respect and confidence when two parties work collaboratively to achieve desired results. Because the process is reciprocal, both the manager and employee benefit by working and interacting together. How can both individuals increase their self-esteem at the same time? It's easy. Since managers have developed an understanding of their employees on a personal level, they know what is important to them. Thus, they select motivational strategies that challenge and stimulate their employees, creating a higher level of trust and honesty which in turn increases employee confidence. As confidence increases, self-esteem increases. Managers benefit by working closely with their employees, observing their growth and development, and the results that they achieve. This increases managers' confidence in their coaching and managing skills, thus increasing their self-esteem.

Self-esteeming is the culmination of all the steps previously accomplished in the synergistic relationship process (i.e., freedom from fear to honesty) and is the primary benefit of building positive working relationships with employees. It is based on collegial partnerships between managers and their employees. This partnership is based on two-way communication, trust, honesty, and interaction, and should be non-judgmental, free of fear, personal, and professional (Gilley & Boughton, 1996). Self-esteeming allows managers the opportunity to better serve their employees through performance coaching, developmental evaluations, performance growth and development activities, and rewarding and recognizing employees' accomplishments and development (see Chapters 4, 5, 6, 7, and 8).

Self-esteeming benefits managers by increasing their involvement with their employees. This can energize managers, motivating and challenging them to become the best managers they can be. Self-esteeming encourages managers to take on increasingly difficult assignments that initiate change within an organization.

As managers interact with employees every day, they are given opportunities to enhance or diminish their self-esteem. To increase employees' self-concepts, managers can utilize one of four sources of growth and development:

- Achievement, accomplishment, and mastery
- Power, control, and influence
- Being cared about and valued
- Acting on values and beliefs (Bradshaw, 1981, p. 23)

Each of these sources provides an opportunity for employees to enhance their self-esteem. The more positive these experience are, the higher self-esteem will rise. We will discuss these sources of growth and development in greater detail in Chapter 7.

Let us illustrate how self-esteeming works on a practical level. A manager of a large manufacturing company assigns one of her employees a project to create a new product line designed to compete in the international marketplace. The manager and employee have a strong, trusting, honest relationship, and have worked together for five years. The manager clearly explains the parameters of the project, its outcomes, time line, quality specifications, and the employee's level of decision-making authority. The employee is now free to assemble a project team to work with and begin the task of designing and developing a new product line. As the employee begins to work on the project several roadblocks emerge, and the employee asks the manager for her assistance in removing them. The manager makes some suggestions for dealing with each of the barriers and reaffirms her confidence in the employee's abilities and skills. Several weeks into the project, the manager asks for an update and provides positive feedback regarding the completion of important tasks. In addition, the manager and employee discuss other upcoming challenges that will affect the project's completion. This activity is repeated several times during the life of the project. At the completion of the project, the manager rewards and recognizes the employee and her team for a job well done. The employee feels great and is appreciative of the assistance, feedback, and recognition received. In return, the employee shares with the manager her appreciation for being allowed to lead such a challenging project and for the support and guidance received. As a result, the working relationship between the manager and employee is dramatically improved. Thus, self-esteeming has been successfully achieved.

Self-esteeming is a process that organizations must strive for and build on. It is one of the basic tenets for organizational effectiveness, and must be encouraged, embraced, and achieved to successfully meet business results.

Professional Development

Another key outcome of a synergistic relationship is professional development. In fact, it is extremely difficult to develop employees without establishing positive working relationships with them. At this point in the relationship process, managers can directly, honestly discuss ways of improving their employees' competencies and skills. Some employees may surprise their managers and tell them things that they were not prepared to address. While such honesty is often difficult to deal with, it helps managers establish a clear and focused developmental direction for employees.

The following example illustrates steps in the synergistic relationship process that create opportunities for professional development. Recently, we helped an organization implement the Synergistic Relationship model in several business units. As the various managers evolved through each of the steps in the model, one manager was quite surprised by a request made by one of her employees. The employee wanted to take over the warehousing of all internal data, which was quite different from what she was doing. Since their relationship had evolved to the "trust" phase and the employee had sufficient competencies to do the job, the manager was willing to give it a try. She laid out a plan that would allow the employee to train a replacement and made a six-month transition plan to her new job. We asked the employee why she made the request and whether she would have made it six months earlier (prior to introducing the Synergistic Relationship model). She said, "It appeared to me that during the last few months my boss [the manager] demonstrated more confidence in my abilities and that it gave me the courage to try something new." She did not think that six months ago she would have made such request because "it was too scary around here back then." We believe that this is a clear example of how creating synergistic relationships can provide professional development opportunities while simultaneously improving organizational effectiveness.

Unfortunately, one problem prevents synergistic relationships from developing. Managers and employees must be willing to engage one another and stop viewing the other as the "enemy." Synergy cannot be fostered as long as managers and employees are skeptical of the other's intentions. If both parties do not want to improve their relationship, most likely it will not happen.

APPLYING THE SYNERGISTIC RELATIONSHIP MODEL

Have you ever had a working relationship blow up on you? Of course you have. So has everyone else. For example, an employee shares something confidential with his or her manager; the manager mistakenly passes some of this information on to another person, expecting that individual to maintain trust and confidence; eventually, the employee discovers the breach of confidentiality and is devastated. Why? Because the manager has violated his or her trust. What should the manager do now? First, look at the model again (Figure 2.1) and observe that the arrows are going in both directions, which means the synergistic relationship process can go in either direction—forward or backward.

When a serious violation of trust occurs, the relationship regresses—sometimes all the way back to the fear stage. In this case, the only thing the manager can do is repair the damage and move the relationship forward. As a first step, the manager should meet with the employee and apologize for his or her inappropriate behavior. If the employee accepts the apology, the manager may continue. Remember, trust has not been reestablished simply because the employee has offered forgiveness. To repair the damage, the manager must work through all the steps as though beginning a new relationship. Sometimes it takes a long time to return to a point where the employee will trust the manager again, but it can be accomplished.

CONCLUSION

Building synergistic relationships is an ongoing, active, and participatory process that requires a great deal of time, energy, and effort. Improved manager–employee relationships leads to greater trust, honesty, commitment, and productivity, yielding emotional and financial rewards for employees, managers, and the organization.

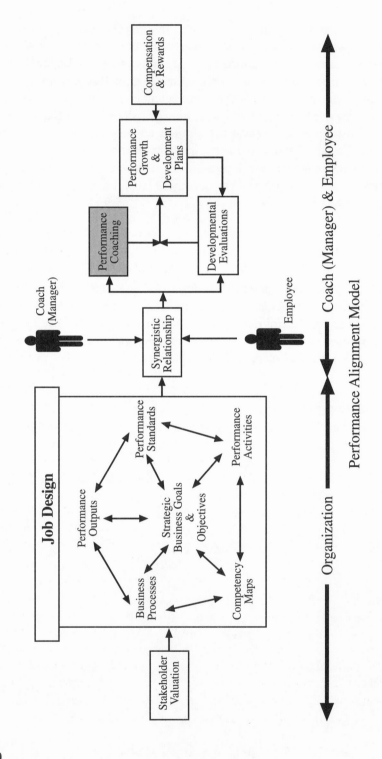

Performance Alignment Model

Chapter 5

APPLYING PERFORMANCE COACHING

The heart of every organization, large or small, manufacturing or service, is its managers. Organizations assign managers the task of securing results through people. They serve as guides, directors, decision makers, and energizers for their employees. They further function as trainers, confronters, counselors, and mentors in an effort to maximize results needed by the organization. Managers are the conduits of organizational change and development; without them, organizations struggle in mediocrity.

Most of us have worked for managers who are abusive and indifferent toward employees, possessing superior attitudes and poor interpersonal skills. We've experienced managers with poor listening and feedback skills, who fail to delegate, develop people, or conduct developmental evaluations. These managers exercise little or no patience with their employees as they struggle to improve performance, and criticize employees' personalities rather than focus on their work performance. We have all been victims of managers who create work environments full of fear and paranoia, and who defy us to challenge their authority. In short, we've all experienced the manager from hell—that individual who exhibits some or all of the above characteristics. As a result, employee morale and productivity remain low, which lead to poor-quality products and services, and higher costs.

As CEOs, board of director members, and senior executives contemplate their organization's future, they often overlook one of the most common problems preventing them from achieving their desired business results: *managerial malpractice*. This problem has plagued organizations for years and has become the Achilles' heel of literally thousands of firms. Neither inadequate planning nor financial management, poor product quality nor service reliability, organizational structure nor its policies and procedures are as widespread. Managerial malpractice is a simple problem that is seldom addressed by organizations—and if left unchecked it will prevent organizations from achieving the effectiveness and efficiency they desire.

Simply stated, managerial malpractice is maintaining and using managers who are unqualified, poorly trained, misguided, or inadequately prepared. These managers do not have the interpersonal skills required to enhance employee commitment and improve organizational performance (Gilley & Boughton, 1996, p. 4).

Most of us have experienced managerial malpractice "up close and personal." But how does one know when one's organization is suffering from managerial malpractice? In Chapter 1, we identified symptoms of managerial malpractice. The daunting question looms: how many of these symptoms are allowed to continue before organizations recognize them as problems? The answer rests in the successful transformation from managing to performance coaching.

Performance coaching begins with the creation of a healthy, positive, synergistic relationship between managers and their employees (see Chapter 4). In Chapter 4, we identified nine components that are critical in creating a synergistic relationship. We examined how these components interact with one another and how they contribute to the formation of a participatory attitude on the part of employees. We discussed how managers use each of these nine components to form a better working relationship with their employees. Once synergistic relationships are established, performance coaches can address the performance challenge.

DEVELOPING FEEDBACK SKILLS

Making the transition from manager to performance coach requires adoption of a performance feedback philosophy. This philosophy is critical to enhancing employee growth and development, as employees cannot perform adequately unless they understand how they are doing.

Performance feedback can be direct or indirect, verbal or written, solicited or unsolicited, and friendly or unfriendly (Gilley & Boughton, 1996). Regardless of its form, feedback is essential to employee growth and development—helping employees know when they are producing the kind of performance outcomes needed by the organization or completing performance activities correctly (see Chapter 3).

Managerial malpractice occurs most frequently when managers fail to provide performance feedback to their employees. Many managers mistakenly believe that their employees know when they are or are not performing correctly. Unfortunately, most do not. Therefore, it is the manager's responsibility to provide clear, concise, sincere, and timely feedback. A good working definition of feedback is "getting timely and specific information about job performance that includes praise or developmental direction." *Timely* means giving feedback on an ongoing basis, not just during annual performance reviews. *Specific* entails documenting exact performance behaviors that can be referenced when giving feedback to an employee. *Praise* and *developmental direction* entail providing feedback that relates to entire job performance. These definitions help entrench a performance coach's feedback philosophy.

Feedback is a powerful motivator and source of encouragement for employees. Providing performance feedback helps managers build synergistic relationships with their employees while reducing conflicts regarding performance. Feedback also helps employees better understand their strengths and weaknesses so that a "development plan" can be created. Giving timely and specific feedback leads to improved business results.

Implementing Performance Feedback

Performance coaches should communicate feedback in a way that encourages employees to improve their performance. Feedback should be delivered positively, thus preventing employees from becoming defensive. It should be ongoing, and not a surprise. That is, performance feedback should reinforce things that employees know about themselves and quickly recognize so they can make minor corrections in their job performance.

Implementing performance feedback requires appropriate and adequate documentation by performance coaches prior to sharing their observations with employees. In other words, leave a paper trail. Recording every incident of performance feedback is unrealistic; however, when observable patterns of poor or good performance exist, record the data. Thorough documentation of poor performance assures objectivity in dealing with the problem and the employee. Accurate documentation of good performance justifies assigning new and challenging work to that employee. Precise, comprehensive documentation will place the performance coach (and the organization) on firm legal footing if an employee's performance leads to termination.

A seven-step process may be utilized by performance coaches to provide their employees with feedback regarding incorrect performance:

Step 1: Demystify the performance problem by telling the employee exactly what was done incorrectly. Whenever possible, provide feedback immediately.

Step 2: Allow the employee to respond to feedback. This requires listening to the employee's response and observing his or her nonverbal behavior.

Step 3: Once the employee's perspective of his or her performance is understood, offer concrete evidence of the poor performance. Be specific and clear in your presentation.

Step 4: Attempt to identify the strength(s) possessed by the employee that may compensate for the weakness in performance. That is, find something that the employee does well that will help overcome the weakness demonstrated.

Step 5: Identify the appropriate performance that the employee can demonstrate. This may include exact steps to be followed, changes to be made, or the way to go about improving or ensuring quality. Either way, your expectations must be clear.

Step 6: Review the downside of continuous poor performance. In other words, you have a responsibility to communicate to the employee the consequences of poor performance (discipline, suspension, termination, etc.). It is your responsibility to make certain the employee understands that poor performance will not be accepted, and that change must be forthcoming.

Step 7: Make certain the employee understands that it is his or her responsibility to correct performance and that he or she has ownership of the problem. The performance coach should help identify ways of improving performance or the skills and knowledge necessary for improvement.

THE PERFORMANCE COACHING PROCESS

Some believe that the performance coaching process is simply a formalized feedback approach. On the contrary, it is a much more complex, complicated process that includes several important roles and activities that managers must adopt in order to help their employees solve problems, improve performance, and achieve desired results.

The performance coaching process is designed to:

- eliminate managerial malpractice (reason 4)
- help organizations better manage performance (reason 5, see Figure 1.2)

At its heart, performance coaching is a person-centered management technique that requires face-to-face communications, personal involvement with employees, and establishment of rapport. This is an active process requiring constant shifts from one role to another. It transforms managers from passive observers into active participants with employees. Performance coaching is based on good questioning, listening, feedback, and facilitation skills as opposed to autocratic, controlling techniques.

Peterson and Hicks (1996) believe that coaching is a continuous process, not an occasional conversation. They contend that coaching is a process of equipping people with the tools, knowledge, and opportunities they need to develop themselves and to be more effective employees (p. 14). Further, they maintain that the performance coaching process allows performance coaches to embark on three uniquely separate frontiers. These include working one on one with employees, guiding employees to learn for themselves, and orchestrating resources and learning opportunities by which employees can maximize their growth and development potential.

Performance coaching occurs whenever and wherever a need arises, bolstering the relationship between managers and employees. Consequently, the foundation of the performance coaching process is the synergistic relationship discussed in Chapter 4.

Observation of employee performance remains the primary information-gathering tool of managers. If an employee performs well, positive reinforcement is appropriate. Failure to perform adequately or to follow proper organization policy/procedure necessitates the manager's responsibility to determine cause and furnish the employee with instructions that will enable successful execution in the future. Performance coaches are also responsible for follow-up; that is, making certain that corrective action has been taken.

The key to effective performance coaching is to handle problem situations without causing resentment on the part of employees. An overzealous manager wishing to demonstrate advanced knowledge of the job or power and superiority over employees easily creates resentment. Consequently, performance coaching is a minute-by-minute, day-by-day activity that replaces the traditional directing, organizing, coordinating, and controlling activities so commonly outlined in most management textbooks.

In order to be an effective performance coach, you must be able to create an environment that brings out the best in employees. To accomplish this, you must be able to meet or exceed the following criteria:

- establish clear performance goals
- provide accurate feedback
- be patient with employees who are experiencing difficulty on the job
- create fear-free environments
- expect success of employees
- encourage excellence
- ask questions
- allow employees to make mistakes and govern their own performance (Gilley & Boughton, 1996, pp. 43–45)

Performance coaches must possess several personal qualities in order to be effective. They must be enthusiastic, self-controlled, impartial, honest, self-confident, genuine, friendly, optimistic, visionary, open-minded, flexible, and resourceful. In addition, effective performance coaches must be willing to accept criticism, maintain a sense of humor, allow others to offer suggestions and recommendations, and be willing to accept employees' successes and failures.

Misperceptions of Performance Coaching

It is a common misconception that performance coaching requires hours and hours of private tutoring with employees. While personal feedback and attention are required for success, the coach's primary responsibility is to create conditions that enable employees to develop on their own. The performance coach is required to spend time training employees; however, the majority of their development should be based on their individualized growth and development plans.

Many believe that coaching is simply a technique for resolving performance problems. While this is an extremely important aspect of the performance coaching process, it comprises only a small portion of the performance coach's time. Later in this chapter we discuss the four primary roles of performance coaches—which clearly indicate that the majority of their time is spent in activities other than corrective behavior.

Performance coaching constitutes more than providing feedback, advice, or recommendations. It is a process that relies on employees' insight into their own behavior and a gentle, effective approach to guiding them to change. Feedback is a cornerstone of performance coaching that requires more advanced interpersonal and communication skills as well as active listening, analysis techniques, and performance analysis interpretations.

Skeptics assert that performance coaching is simply the newest management development fad. However, leaders throughout history have used coaching techniques to develop and enhance performance capacity. These techniques have been employed to help employees adapt to change and adjust their performance on the job. Peterson and Hicks (1996) contend that performance coaching equips people to develop themselves. Similarly, an old Chinese proverb states "give a man a fish you feed him for a day, teach a man to fish you feed him for a lifetime." The same is true of the performance coaching process. It is indeed a continuous developmental activity.

Purpose of the Performance Coaching Process

As stated previously, the performance coaching process is designed to help improve employee performance, solve problems, and secure desired organizational results. Improving performance is a five-stage process, which begins by identifying the performance outputs required and communicating them to employees. Performance outputs are the business results required by the organization—from corporate profitability to the number of successful claims processed by a claims adjuster. In short, performance outputs are the deliverables that employees are paid to produce.

The second stage is identifying the employee's performance activities required to produce a given output. Performance activities include the step-by-step tasks or engagements (processes) necessary to produce a product or service. Performance activities reflect the best practices an employee will use on the job.

The third stage involves identifying performance standards that must be met or exceeded regarding performance outputs or activities. These standards serve as criteria to be used when determining whether a performance output has been produced at an acceptable level or whether a job has been completed correctly. They also serve as a blueprint in executing the job task or providing performance deliverables.

The fourth stage entails comparing an employee's current performance with established standards, which is done at both the performance output and activity levels. This step determines whether there is a serious deviation in the execution of a given job or a difference between actual performance outputs and desired outputs. Regardless of the outcome, a record should be kept for future reference and to serve as a baseline for performance improvement.

After a performance evaluation has been conducted, the final stage of improving performance begins. If a deficiency exists in output or activities, changes must be made in order to improve the way a job is being performed or outputs are being created. Changes may include new policies, procedures, or processes for executing performance activities, or establishing new ways of producing performance outputs.

In some situations, actual performance exceeds performance standards. When this condition occurs, it is still important to examine possible ways to improve productivity in order to ensure that high levels of performance continue. If no significant difference exists between actual and desired performance, it may still be appropriate to make adjustments to ensure continuous improvement.

Another purpose of performance coaching is to help employees solve problems. Performance coaches can employ alternative problem-solving techniques that include:

- identifying the problem
- isolating the root cause of the problem
- identifying possible solutions
- analyzing solutions
- selecting a solution
- implementing the solution
- evaluating the solution

This approach has a proven track record, yet it is important to remember that it is the employees' responsibility to integrate the problem-solving process on the job (see Chapter 10). They must be taught how to effectively execute each step of the process. In this way, problem solving becomes the responsibility *of* employees rather than a technique employed *for* them.

Perhaps the most important aspect of the performance coaching process is helping the organization achieve the results it needs. Desired results can include increasing sales, obtaining more units of productivity, improving customer service, or raising market share. Managers cannot obtain desired results by themselves—they rely on their employees. This is where classic management techniques begin to fall apart, as directing, organizing, and controlling employees may not produce positive results. Fortunately, making the transformation from manager to performance coach offers the process necessary for securing results through people.

PERFORMANCE COACHING CONTINUUMS

Different situations require different coaching styles. Managers must be able to recognize varying situations and adapt to the behaviors and needs of employees. There is a time to be directive and assertive with employees, while at other times a supportive, amiable approach is more appropriate. Simultaneously, certain situations require clear demonstration of leadership, while others call for operation as a performance partner for purposes of guaranteeing satisfactory organizational results.

Coaching opportunities generally call for behaviors that fall along two continuums (Figure 5.1). These two continuums can be combined to create a working relationship that illustrates the possible performance coaching roles encountered with employees. The horizontal continuum reveals assertive/supportive behavior with employees, while the vertical continuum expresses leader/partner behavior.

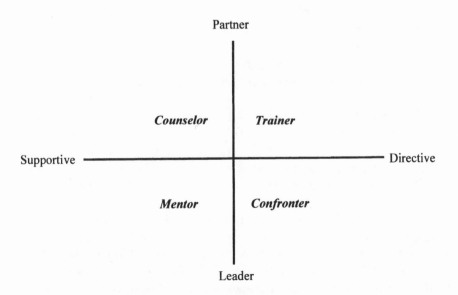

Figure 5.1 Performance Coaching Continuums

This model illustrates four primary roles, each of which represents philosophical orientation toward performance coaching. For example, providing instruction, feedback, and confrontation requires the directive approach with employees—which can be represented by the training and confronting roles of performance coaching. Other situations require a supportive approach, represented by the mentoring and counseling roles. Further definition of roles depends on the coach's perception of whether to serve as a leader or partner with employees. Each role has a number of different outcomes associated with it. Each will be briefly explained, with common outcomes identified.

Trainer

Performance coaching is characterized by several critical roles, one of the most important being that of trainer. As trainers, performance coaches are directive, but operate as partners in performance improvement using feedback and summary techniques to make certain that employees fully grasp the concepts being taught (Figure 5.1). When employees do not possess the knowledge, skills, or attitudes to appropriately perform their jobs, or when they are unable to properly sequence performance activities and tasks, it is appropriate for performance coaches to serve in the role of trainer. In this role, the coach serves as a one-on-one tutor with employees, responsible for sharing information that will ultimately impact employee growth and development. This traditionally comes in the form of on-the-job training, but can also include formal training activities.

In the training role, managers should only present information that is meaningful as well as practical to their employees—and in a way that permits mastery. Employees must understand completely and be able to utilize their training in order for it to be meaningful. This may require the trainer to present one idea or concept at a time, often sequentially, rather than explaining the whole performance process in its entirety. To be an effective trainer a performance coach must use feedback with frequent summaries to make certain that information has been understood by employees.

As trainers, performance coaches guide and direct employees, helping them in the acquisition of knowledge, skills, and appropriate attitudes. To be successful as trainers, performance coaches must utilize the communication process between themselves and their employees to demonstrate how additional knowledge, skills, and attitudes can help produce desired outcomes.

In its simplest sense, training can be thought of as the communication of experience. Experience may involve demonstrating how a specific skill improves the completion of a task or how new knowledge enables employees to better problem solve or analyze a performance situation. It is most appropriate when employees:

- don't have the knowledge or skills to do their jobs (reason 8)
- don't know how to do their jobs (reason 9)
- don't understand their job responsibilities (reason 10, see Figure 1.3).

When these circumstances are present, performance coaches should focus on training activities that break down complicated tasks into small, manageable steps that enable a less-experienced employee to master them. Employees then learn how to perform tasks one step at a time. If training is successful, employees will be able to perform the tasks adequately.

Training is a very complex, complicated process requiring great skill and expertise. To master the role of trainer, performance coaches must incorporate three distinct elements into every training activity:

- arrange the training environment to maximize opportunities to communicate privately and without interruption
- communicate in language easily understood by employees
- present information one step at a time, allowing employees to apply the task or skills under realistic conditions; allow time for review, reflection, and evaluation

Confronter

There are times when employees fail to perform their jobs adequately. Under these conditions, performance coaches serve as confronters—they are very directive and leader-oriented (Figure 5.1). In this role, the coach's entire attention is focused on resolving performance problems. The greatest benefit to the organization can be gleaned via the execution of this role. Benefits include improved quality, efficiency, and productivity that lead to enhanced organizational performance capacity. These improvements ultimately enhance the organization's competitiveness in the marketplace, which can lead to greater market share and higher profits.

As confronters, performance coaches are responsible for identifying and addressing their employees' performance shortfalls. This is accomplished by identifying performance standards, communicating them to employees, comparing actual work to desired standards, and discussing results with employees. When performance falls short of standards, coaches must determine why their employees are failing to perform adequately. Several possible reasons exist for inadequate employee performance:

- they think there is a better way of doing their jobs (reason 11)
- they are not confronted upon failure to perform their jobs correctly (reason 12)
- they refuse to produce performance outcomes required (reason 13, Figure 1.3)

Once reasons are identified, performance coaches must use their confronting skills to identify possible barriers or conflicts in the work environment that prevent or discourage their employees' adequate execution of tasks and responsibilities. By identifying and resolving these barriers or conflicts, coaches enable employees to perform at the highest possible level of efficiency.

Many performance coaches have difficulty confronting employees who do not perform adequately. Many avoid the situation, hoping that somehow, miraculously, the situation will improve on its own, without having to confront employees. When these managers do finally get around to confronting their employees, they tend to overdo it by making personal statements rather than by focusing on the performance problem. As a result, conflict arises, things are said, and emotions are expressed that produce hurt feelings and resentment. Furthermore, job performance doesn't really improve. Consequently, many relationships are frayed and managers are even more reluctant to confront employees in the future.

To overcome this dilemma, performance coaches must know the difference between confrontation and criticism (Figure 5.2). When a coach confronts employees, the focus must be on the performance problem and its results. The underlying problem must be specific, and possible solutions offered for correction. Confronting is future-oriented, focusing on realistic changes that employees can implement. Finally, performance confronting should enhance the relationship between coaches and employees in such a way that employees feel confident in discussing future job performance difficulties.

Criticism, on the other hand, focuses on the person and his or her

Confronting	Criticizing
Problem Focuses on the problem, giving concrete, objective facts: "The record shows that you have been late three days in this pay period."	**Person** Focuses on the person and his or her attitude or traits: "Your laziness in getting to work on time is causing problems."
Specific Identifies specifically what should occur or change; starts with the most recent example: "Your time card shows that you were late again today. Your team needs to be on the job by eight."	**General** Uses general statements that may magnify the problem by using words like *never, always,* or *continually:* "You're always letting me down no matter how hard I try to help you."
Change Focuses on the future and what can be changed, not on making the team member feel guilty, weak, or pessimistic. Encourages employees to want to change: "I'd like to come up with a plan so that you can do better next time."	**Blame** Establishes blame, making the team member feel guilty and focusing on the past: "You leave your equipment out every night. What's so important that you can't stop to put things in order?"
Relationship Focuses on improving performance, increasing commitment, and building positive work relationships: "I'd like to help you meet your goal next time. What solutions do you suggest?"	**Self** Centers on the needs of the critic himself or herself and sometimes involves venting that person's anger or frustration: "Your behavior really embarrasses me! It makes me look like a bad leader."

Figure 5.2 Confrontation versus Criticism

attitudes or traits. In many cases, these characteristics are not based on observable facts, but on the perceptions a manager holds of the employee and the way work tasks are accomplished. Another characteristic of criticism is that its nature prohibits the employee from focusing on the specific problem at hand. Broad statements such as *never, always,* or *continually* are often used to describe employees' performance difficulties, but rarely are specific examples, circumstances, or situations provided to the employee as a way of focusing attention. Criticism epitomizes blaming behavior that allows inadequate managers to project negative feelings toward their employees or to fix blame for difficulties they created due to their poor management skills. Finally, criticism is a self-serving, self-centered, counterproductive activity that allows the critic to vent anger or frustration toward another individual.

In order for employees to enhance their personal growth, commit to continuous performance improvement, and accept increasingly difficult tasks and responsibilities, performance coaches must master the art of confronting. According to Gilley and Boughton (1996) three critical skill sets are required of a successful performance confronter: (1) assertion skills, (2) conflict resolution skills, and (3) collaborative problem-solving skills.

Assertion skills utilize nonjudgmental descriptions of the performance behaviors to be changed. Assertion skills require performance coaches to disclose their feelings regarding their employees' behavior, making a general disclosure of the emotions felt as a result of experiencing this behavior. The easiest way to express feelings regarding unacceptable behavior is to use "I" messages such as "I feel . . ." to describe what's going on inside. "I" messages are shared with employees to allow them to understand the effects of inadequate performance. Following are examples of nonjudgmental behavioral descriptions, disclosure of feelings, and their verification and effects. "When you are frequently late for work . . . I feel angry . . . because it costs us money to delay the production line." "When you overspend your budget . . . I feel annoyed . . . because it means I must make cuts that will affect the quality of the project" (Gilley & Boughton, 1996, p. 152).

Conflict resolution skills enable performance coaches to deal with the turbulence that typically causes conflict. They include acknowledging and clarifying conflict, problem solving with employees, and confirming solutions. This process involves a set of skills that help performance coaches govern conflict. Conflict resolution is a constructive process for handling emotion-laden disagreements between coaches and their employees. This process encourages assertive communication and a sharing of feelings, but does not permit the typical free-for-all that blocks creative resolution of conflict and tends to be very destructive to relationships.

Collaborative problem-solving skills include ways of resolving conflicts and problems that will satisfy performance coaches, their employees, and the organization. Many conflicts within organizations occur because of unresolved needs or those that are in conflict with one another. Therefore, performance coaches should use a collaborative problem-solving approach, previously discussed, to address and satisfy employee needs.

Mentor

There are times when performance coaches will find it necessary to be supportive and serve as leaders with employees, performing the role of mentor (Figure 5.1). Mentoring encourages performance coaches to share their experiences with employees, helping employees gain additional insight, understanding, and awareness that will be invaluable in the progression of their careers. Mentoring allows employees to benefit from coaches' experiences, both the successes and failures, thus alleviating employees fears, concerns, frustrations, and pains while promoting celebration of successes, victories, and job accomplishments. By its supportive, interactive nature, mentoring helps performance coaches become more caring, sympathetic, and patient. In short, via mentoring, developing employees helps performance coaches grow as well.

Mentoring is a process of ultimate sharing, providing performance coaches the opportunity to unlock the mysteries of the organization for their mentees (Gilley & Boughton, 1996). Mentoring helps employees avoid the costly mistakes and pitfalls so damaging to their careers. It can also help employees adjust to the firm's culture and better assimilate into the organizational work environment.

Traditional managers who maintain an authoritative, uninvolved style based on the "my way or the highway" mentality have difficulty performing as mentors. Performance coaches who value their relationships with their employees and strive to overcome managerial malpractice can make excellent mentors. Mentoring, more than any other role, requires that performance coaches develop a synergistic, self-esteeming relationship with their employees. They must also believe that the success of the organization is based on the success of its employees. When these attitudes are present, performance coaches function effectively as mentors—and are well on the road to overcoming the performance challenge.

To be effective mentors, performance coaches must have substantial knowledge of the organization, including thorough understanding of its vision, direction, and long-range goals and objectives. They must also maintain an appropriate network that will enable employees to make critical contacts throughout the organization. Successful mentors possess and share technical competence to help employees overcome skill deficiencies. Most successful mentors possess a degree of charisma; employees are drawn to individuals who possess the ability to persuade others, and like to be around people whose opinions and ideas are sought by other members of the organization. Mentors must have credibility within the organization. Finally, to be effective mentors performance coaches must be willing to bear responsibility for someone else's growth and development. At the heart of a mentoring relationship is an eagerness to improve employees and help them become the best that they can be.

As mentors, performance coaches render several activities for employee growth and development. As a result, mentors often serve as confidants in times of personal and professional difficulty, providing feedback, observation of performance, and personal responses. Mentors provide insight about the mission, goals, and strategic direction of an organization. They help employees develop political savvy and awareness that enable them to function efficiently and effectively within the organization. Mentors provide employees with insights into organizational philosophy, operations, and the functional system. They help employees with long-term career planning, advocating for growth, encouraging risk taking, and providing advancement opportunities. Mentors enable their employees to participate in visible projects and programs that may further advance their careers. Finally, mentors serve as honest, open, direct advisors.

Counselor

Certain circumstances call for performance coaches to partner with their employees, while encouraging employees to make independent decisions (supporter) (Figure 5.1). These conditions require performance coaches to serve in the role of counselor. As a counselor, the performance coach's primary responsibility is to help employees uncover underlying assumptions regarding their careers, and help them analyze reasons for their current career plans. As a counselor, the performance coach poses hypothetical questions to employees to expand their perspectives regarding their careers. They help employees examine their commitment to their careers, often presenting differing viewpoints in order to help them develop a more in-depth analysis of career options and decisions.

As a counselor, the performance coach helps employees make better career decisions and helps the organization better allocate human resources. Counselors help employees gain greater insight into the organization, enhance their self-sufficiency, and better understand their feelings regarding their careers.

In order to be successful as counselors, performance coaches must shift their managerial style from authoritative to participatory. Performance coaches must relinquish control and dominance over their employees, allowing them to participate as equal partners in examining their careers, performance problems, or difficulties. A participatory approach requires that performance coaches develop positive working relationships with employees. These relationships develop when performance coaches recognize that their employees bring a great deal of experience and talent to the organization, and are invaluable assets to be acknowledged, tapped, and improved.

The participatory approach is relatively nonthreatening to employees, requiring their active involvement in problem solving. Participation encourages employees to support the decisions made and the solutions recommended, enabling the free exchange of ideas, opinions, and feelings. Employees benefit from positive communications climates as they feel more secure and can freely express their thoughts and ideas. This climate is considered comfortable and conducive to sharing, even nurturing to employee development. A sharing climate goes beyond the superficial to demonstrate a deep concern for the well-being of employees, and is dedicated to the improvement of interpersonal relations (Gilley & Boughton, 1996, p. 132).

Once performance coaches have created an open communications environment, the stage is set for them to be counselors. Now is the time to utilize their interpersonal communication skills, which can be grouped into three categories. The first are *relationship* skills that demonstrate concern for employees, including attentiveness, empathy, genuineness, nonverbal techniques, rapport, and understanding (see Chapter 4). These skills create trust and fearlessness in employees. Performance coaches must also have *following* skills that give them the discipline to let employees analyze their own problems and identify solutions. Following skills comprise two major areas: (1) active listening, in which performance coaches are more interested in what employees have to say than hearing their own voices, and (2) questioning to clarify employee statements rather than assert the performance coach's own opinions (see Chapter 4). Finally, *reflecting* skills cause the employee to rethink, reconsider, and reprocess information. Techniques such as clarifying, interpreting, and summarizing feelings and thoughts are reflective. Once performance coaches have summarized employees' thoughts and feelings, they can help employees determine the most appropriate steps for resolving performance problems and career issues.

SELF-ESTEEMING AND SECURING RESULTS THROUGH REWARDS

The last two steps of the performance coaching process are developing self-esteeming employees and getting results through people. These two components of the performance coaching process will be addressed in Chapters 7 and 8, respectively. Here, we provide a short overview.

Performance coaches help employees develop self-esteem by

providing challenging and rewarding assignments, positive feedback, and encouragement. Self-esteeming is a process in which performance coaches and their employees complement one another, and the whole of the relationship is greater than the sum of its parts. Self-esteeming is also based on the enormously powerful need to feel good about one's self and the experiences, skills, and abilities one possesses. In short, self-esteeming is the sum total of how employees feel about themselves.

Ultimately, the performance coaching process is self-esteeming, based on a collegial partnership between performance coaches and their employees. Self-esteeming provides performance coaches with an opportunity to better serve their employees through training, confronting, mentoring, and counseling. These roles help employees improve their self-concepts (self-esteem), which leads to improved organizational performance. Consequently, self-esteeming is a developmental process by which employees grow, enhance their performance, and advance their careers (see Chapter 6).

The primary purpose of any organization is to achieve desired business results. For some, desired results could include increased revenue, improved quality, greater market share, or increased profitability. Regardless, it is the responsibility of performance coaches and their employees to achieve the results needed by the organization.

The ultimate purpose of the performance coaching process is to help managers get results through people. Each of the four roles previously discussed will help performance coaches resolve problems, improve performance, and, most important, achieve desired results. In order to successfully achieve desired outcomes, it is important to identify reward strategies (monetary or nonmonetary) that encourage employee commitment and involvement. In this way, performance coaches can link compensation and rewards to employee performance growth and development plans (see Chapter 8).

Improving performance, resolving problems, and achieving desired business results is a complex, difficult process. Performance coaches must identify rewards that motivate employees to accomplish these outcomes. This is a simple philosophy—one that is often misunderstood and abused in today's organizations.

INTERFACE OF PERFORMANCE COACHING COMPETENCIES AND THE PERFORMANCE ALIGNMENT PROCESS

Figure 5.3 identifies phases of the performance alignment process that constitute performance-coaching competencies. They include the syner-

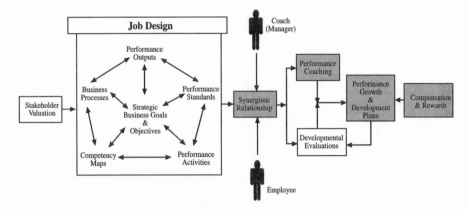

Figure 5.3 Interface of Performance Coaching Competencies and Performance Alignment Process

gistic relationship, performance coaching (the four roles), self-esteeming process (creating performance growth and development plans), and linking compensation and rewards to employee performance growth and development. These four phases of the performance alignment process consist of seven separate but distinct competencies. We have developed the Performance Coaching Inventory (PCI), which is a self-assessment instrument to help managers identify their performance coaching competencies (see Appendix).

CONCLUSION

Successful organizations have managers who motivate and inspire their employees, not discourage or beat them down. These individuals see themselves not just as "bosses" but as performance coaches, taking the responsibility for: (1) providing employees with training that applies directly to the job, (2) helping employees enhance their careers and solve problems, (3) confronting employees in positive ways to improve performance, and (4) mentoring employees to help them become the best they can be. The result is motivated, productive employees ready to accept challenges and take initiative. This process is based on the synergistic relationship between performance coaches and their employees, and is designed to enhance their self-esteem and productivity.

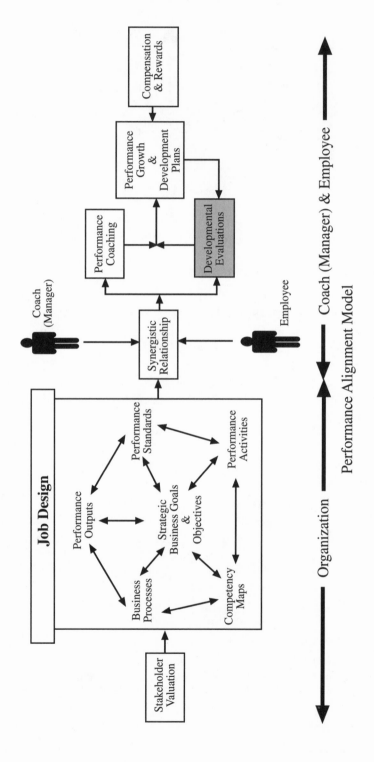

Performance Alignment Model

Chapter 6

CONDUCTING DEVELOPMENTAL EVALUATIONS

One of the most important activities in which organizations can engage to overcome the performance challenge is to conduct regular (monthly, quarterly, semiannual, or annual) performance appraisals with every employee. Performance appraisals, often called performance reviews, give managers the opportunity to judge the adequacy and quality of employees' performance and create growth and development plans that improve their performance. Unfortunately, the term "performance appraisal" restricts the manager's ability to work collaboratively with employees in their development. To overcome this problem, we refer to performance appraisals as developmental evaluations.

Developmental evaluations provide an excellent tool for determining whether employees are producing adequate performance outputs and executing performance activities that meet or exceed performance standards (reason 13, see Figure 1.3). Developmental evaluations should be used to ascertain satisfaction of internal and external stakeholders with performance outputs produced by employees.

One of the primary activities of a developmental evaluation is to assess employees' strengths and weaknesses. In this way, developmental evaluations provide managers (performance coaches) with opportunities to analyze employees' knowledge, skills, and attitudes, and to determine areas of excellence or those needing improvement. These evaluations also present opportunities for performance coaches and employees to discuss current and future developmental goals and objectives, and how employees plan to achieve them. Most important, developmental evaluations are a vehicle for discussion of future growth and development activities that will enhance employees' abilities and competencies as well as advance their careers (see Chapter 7).

Developmental evaluations are an excellent tool for analyzing employee performance and making recommendations for improvement. Many employees fail to perform adequately due to barriers that prohibit exemplary performance (Gilley, 1998). Developmental evaluations help isolate these obstacles and formulate strategies for overcoming them. As a result of these conversations, employees participate in discussions that improve the work environment and general conditions under which they are asked to perform. Furthermore, employees can participate in analysis of job design and assist in identification of improvements and efficiencies in the execution of job tasks.

At the core of every developmental evaluation lies the concept of feedback. In this way, developmental evaluations and performance coaching are very similar activities. The fundamental difference between the two is that performance coaching is an ongoing, minute-by-minute, day-by-day feedback opportunity, while developmental evaluations are designed to be formal, summative evaluations. In some respects, both performance coaching and developmental evaluations are designed to achieve the same end: the creation of growth and development plans that improve employee performance. Consequently, developmental evaluations must be specific and timely in order for employees to make the types of corrections and improvements required to bring about desired business results.

If employees lack the feedback needed to make appropriate corrections, they will be "flying blind" without any kind of assistance from the organization. As a result, they will make decisions regarding their performance without adequate data. Lacking necessary data, employees will make mistakes—their decisions may have disastrous results. Without feedback employees don't know where they are, how they're doing, or whether they're producing satisfactory results. Unless performance coaches tell them, employees don't know if they're producing results on time, at the correct level of quality, or in the proper form. In the final analysis, developmental evaluations give performance coaches the opportunity to share their perspectives of their employees' performance and discuss means of improvement. In this way, developmental evaluations serve a vital function within the organization.

As previously discussed, developmental evaluations provide employees with feedback on their performance, identify their strengths and achievements over a specific period of time, demonstrate areas where they can continue to grow and develop, define performance goals for the next six months to a year, and review the "fit" between the organization's expectations and those of employees. In essence, developmental evaluations help organizations make decisions regarding the performance of employees and aid in construction of developmental and career planning activities that enhance their work. (Designing and constructing growth and development plans will be discussed in greater detail in Chapter 7.)

TYPES OF DEVELOPMENTAL EVALUATIONS

Gilley and Davidson (1993) created a framework that serves as a planning tool when conducting developmental evaluations. They identified five different types of appraisal opportunities, each of which differs in application, focus, purpose, manager's role, employee's role, and power distribution (Figure 6.1). The types of developmental activities include work planning and review, compensation review, developmental planning, career planning, and human resource planning. As you can see from the information provided in Figure 6.1, these activities differ significantly in their execution and intent. They are designed for specific outcomes, requiring managers and employees to constantly shift roles. The degree to which employees and managers share power is also illustrated. This framework helps determine which type of developmental evaluation activity is the most appropriate to conduct with employees. Furthermore, the framework serves as a guide in the execution of each of the different types of developmental evaluations.

Work Planning and Reviews

The purpose of work planning and review is to direct, control, and improve performance. Its focus is on an individual's current job and is designed to manage workflow by objectives and results. In this situation, the manager's role is that of an authoritative figure designed to be "the boss" while the employee's role is that of subordinate. Power and authority in this type of review process is 90 percent manager-oriented and 10 percent employee. Work planning and review activities are closely aligned with the activities conducted during the performance coaching process—most notably, in the confronting role of the performance coach. They have a place in developmental evaluation in that they can be used as a formal activity as well as an ongoing, daily event. Work planning and reviews are characterized by discussions between managers and employees about the goals and objectives employees are attempting to achieve and the results they are attempting to accomplish. Short in duration, usually ten to fifteen minutes, sometimes as much as one-half to one hour, they allow time for the free flow of information.

Point of Contact → / How It Works ↓	Work Planning and Review	Compensation Review	Developmental Planning	Career Planning	Human Resource Planning
In Other Words	• Management of objectives • Management by results • Performance appraisals	• Salary review • Merit increases • Bonuses • Benefits and nonmonetary rewards	• Planning for self-improvement and growth • Action planning	• Determining career interests • Setting career goals • Taking the "long view" • Life planning: career counselor	• Continuity or organizational • High potential career planning • Succession planning • Career pathing
Focus	Job	Rewards	Skills	**POTENTIAL** Individual	Organization
Purpose	**Direct and Control Performance** • Traditional work supervision	**Motivation** • Reward worker for past performance • Motivate worker for future performance	**Improve Personal Skills** • Knowledge • Attitude • On-the-job skills	**Identify Goals** • Determine career goals and clarify career plans	**Maintain Organizational Continuity**
Manager's Role	**Boss** Manager should be assertive and forthright.	**Judge** Manager should evaluate performance and provide rational for decision.	**Consultant** Manager provides insights about worker skills and potential; suggests ways to develop and where to focus efforts.	**Advisor** Manager shares knowledge about organization, personal experience, etc.; makes worker aware of choices available, possible future, etc.	**Planner** "What's best for the company as a whole?"
Employee's Role	**Subordinate** Employee should accept direction and advice.	**Salesperson** Can vary from active to passive, but always concerned that accomplishments and performance be noticed and hopefully rewarded.	**Initiator** Employee should be proactive regarding the career options	**Owner** Employee assembles information, weighs alternatives and makes a personal choice.	**Resource** Employee should provide advice and recommendations.
Power	**Manager** 90% but room for employee input.	**Manager** 70% or more, but room for negotiation.	**Balanced Input** 50% from both parties.	**Employee** 100% ultimate decision rests with employee.	**Manager** 100% some employee input, but manager makes final decision.

Figure 6.1 Types of Employee Reviews

Compensation Reviews

Compensation reviews are intended to motivate employees by rewarding past efforts and identifying future compensation and reward potential for upcoming performance. The focus is on identifying the compensation and rewards an employee will receive as a result of meeting or exceeding performance standards. They are characterized by review of salary structure, merit increases, bonuses, benefits, and nonmonetary rewards that are appropriate based on an employee's past and anticipated future performance. The manager's role in compensation review is to serve as judge, deciding the type and amount of reward an employee will receive based on a predetermined set of criteria. The employee functions like a salesperson, occasionally attempting to persuade the supervisor of accomplishments, while sometimes passively receiving information regarding the kind of compensation and reward increase that is appropriate. In this type of review process, the manager exerts less power and authority than during a work planning and review, often leaving room for negotiation with the employee, depending on the strength of their relationship.

Developmental Planning

Developmental planning's purpose is to improve employees' knowledge, skills, and attitudes. The focus of this evaluation is on skill building, and it is characterized by preparing self-improvement and personal growth activities and action planning. During a development planning review managers provide insight into workers' skills, offering suggestions for improvement and where to focus their efforts. In this way, managers serve as consultants to employees. Employees act as initiators, attempting to influence and impact the kind of development activities in which they will engage. Shared power and authority between employees and performance coaches characterize developmental planning evaluations. As a result, agreed-on growth and development plans begin to surface.

Career Planning

Career planning is the process of establishing individual career objectives for employees and creatively developing long-term developmental activities to achieve them. Career planning differs from growth and development plans in the time frame encompassing maximization of knowledge, skills, and abilities. Career planning is a long-term improvement effort (three to five years) while growth and development plans focus on the current job assignment. In short, career planning is a long-term process of charting an employee's career, while growth and development plans help improve employee production immediately. Both activities are developmental in nature and extremely important in the enhancement of employee competencies. Growth and development plans and career planning activities require skillful coordination to improve results and eliminate duplication of effort.

The focus of career planning, therefore, is on the individual. Performance coaches share their knowledge of the organization, personal experience, and career strategies to help make employees aware of their choices. Employees serve as owners during this type of review process in that they assemble information, weigh alternatives, and make career decisions. Employees historically direct this evaluation activity in that they make the ultimate determination regarding their careers.

Human Resource Planning

The most complex developmental planning is that of human resource planning. This activity maintains organizational continuity vis-à-vis human resources over an extended period of time, focusing on career pathing, succession planning, and blending high potential career actions. The performance coach's related responsibility is that of strategic planner, attempting to address the question, "What's best for the company as a whole?" Employees serve as valuable resources during these activities, providing input and insight as requested. Human resource planning remains largely the exclusive domain of managers and executives, with limited solicited employee input. Ultimately, the final human resource determination lies with the organization.

Each of the five developmental evaluations is a separate appraisal opportunity and should not be used in combination as their purpose differs greatly. The amount of time and energy spent in the actual evaluation process varies as well. The most common evaluations that are mistakenly combined are those of work planning and compensation review. Since work-planning evaluations are conducted to direct, control, and improve performance they should not be combined with discussions related to an employee's compensation and rewards. Compensation and reward evaluations should be separate activities used to reward employees for past performance achievements and to motivate future accomplishments. All too often, these two distinct reviews are completed in combination. Consequently, employees enter the developmental evaluation process solely interested in the identification of their future compensation and rewards. This bias prevents open, honest discussions about current or future performance and prohibits an in-depth analysis of strengths and weaknesses. Employees enter this evaluation process anticipating the amount of salary increase or potential bonuses to be received as a result of their performance. Examination of each of the five unique developmental evaluation activities reveals that they are conducted for very different reasons while focusing on distinct activities and outcomes. Thus, it is inappropriate to combine them, as their individual effectiveness is weakened.

CONDUCTING PRE-REVIEW ACTIVITIES

While developmental evaluations differ in their focus and purpose, they share some simple, straightforward principles that, when adhered to, make each and every review activity a success. These include:

1. prepare wisely
2. set performance-related goals, objectives, and outcomes
3. avoid surprises
4. coach (confront), don't criticize
5. document carefully
6. set the developmental evaluation in action

Following these simple principles ensures better preparation and organization, more accurate focus, and specific outcome orientation, all of which promote the success of developmental evaluations regardless of their intent.

Preparing for a developmental evaluation of any type requires thorough analysis, documentation, and review of content. According to Beatty (1989), "the systematic collection of job-related information for each unique job should include *what* is to be done (physical or mental), *how* the job is to be done (tools, equipment, methods, judgments, calculations, etc.), and *why* it is to be done (overall purpose and why the tasks relate one to another)" (p. 182). Several data collection methods can be used for job analysis:

Task analysis is an activity designed to determine the component tasks that comprise a job.

Critical incidents are used to identify important dimensions of a job and describe behaviors that comprise poor, average, or exemplary performance.

Best practices is a qualitative approach used to identify exemplary skills, knowledge, abilities, and practices involved in executing a specific job.

In addition to these types of analyses, data should be gathered from several supplemental sources. Each data source reveals information regarding the employee's current and past performance, developmental activities, work samples, and possible barriers to performance execution. Potential sources of intelligence include:

- feedback from clients or peers regarding employee performance
- time and financial records to support accomplishments
- training or professional activities in which the employee participated
- work samples representative of the employee's performance
- performance barriers that may prevent the employee from producing appropriate outputs
- performance goals or expectations established during previous developmental evaluations

It might be helpful to think of developmental evaluations as a pyramid whose base exemplifies supporting data (Figure 6.2). In this way, the pre-review process enables wise preparation and the setting of performance-related goals and objectives for the developmental evaluation process.

DANGER, DANGER, WILL ROBINSON!

Prior to conducting a developmental evaluation, managers should carefully consider seven questions employees are challenged to answer. Failure to do so has dangerous consequences. These questions focus developmental evaluations, preventing verbal "free-for-alls" common during unplanned performance appraisals. These seven questions represent the most prevalent employee concerns, and are likely to surface during the developmental evaluation:

1. How am I doing?
2. What can I do to improve?

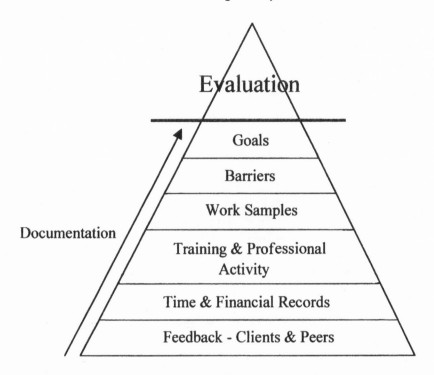

Figure 6.2 Pre-review Process for Gathering Data for the Developmental Evaluation

3. Do I have a chance for advancement?
4. What will be expected of me prior to my next developmental evaluation?
5. How can my work be evaluated during this time?
6. What kind of help or attention can I expect from my manager or supervisor?
7. What changes are likely to occur within the organization that affect my job or performance in the months ahead, and how will they affect me?

Each of these questions should be carefully reviewed prior to entering the evaluation process. Responses should be thoughtfully prepared beforehand in order to be clear, concise, and specific. Employees will feel as though their evaluation has been adequately prepared for, with their performance analysis and developmental suggestions given serious time and consideration. Such courtesy and respect enhance managers' relationships with employees.

In preparation for developmental evaluation engagements, managers should address a number of their own questions. Each will help the manager better prepare for a substantive, outcome-based evaluation. They also serve to outline and direct discussion during the meeting:

1. Have I compared the employee's performance outputs and activities with identified performance standards?
2. What specific performance outputs or activities can I praise the employee for?
3. In what specific areas do I want the employee to improve?
4. Can I support my evaluation of the employee's performance with facts?
5. What specific improvement(s) do I want to see as a result of the evaluation meeting?
6. What kind of professional development activities can I offer my employee?
7. What kind of follow-up do I have planned?
8. What type of growth and development plan would I recommend for this employee?

Developmental evaluations are only as good as the evaluator. Thus, it is important to consider the possible biases managers bring to the evaluation process. While these can be positive or negative in nature, they nevertheless produce a distorted, erroneous view of the employee, his or her performance, or career opportunities. Biases can affect any or all of the five different evaluation reviews and must be guarded against at all times to prevent unsubstantiated, poorly representative evaluations. These biases were first introduced by George Odiorne in his 1965 classic, *Management by Objectives*. He referred to them as the *halo* and *horn* effects of evaluation bias.

Halo Effect

The halo effect is the tendency by a manager or supervisor to overrate a favored employee, which can occur for a variety of reasons:

1. *recency*—allowing a recent event to distort judgment of the employee's entire performance
2. *blind spot effect*—overlooking performance deficiencies because the manager likes the employee for certain activities that he or she performs

3. *compatibility*—overlooking negative performance because an individual is easy to work with, has a pleasing manner, or has a highly desired personality
4. *previous outstanding performance*—previous success overshadows current performance
5. *similar to me*—rating a person highly due to perceived similarities to oneself
6. *favoritism*—allowing poor performance to be overshadowed by qualities the manager personally finds appealing in the employee
7. *overemphasis*—giving too much weight to one outstanding factor, good or bad
8. *no complaint bias*—a "middle-of-the-road" employee has received no negative criticisms or complaints (i.e., no news is good news)
9. *one-asset person*—certain characteristics such as advanced degrees or impressive appearance may be ranked higher than work performance
10. *high potential effect*—persons who *could* achieve or accomplish a great deal are given undue consideration

Horn Effect

The horn effect is the opposite of the halo effect—the tendency to rate a person lower than circumstances justify. Some specific examples include:

1. *grouping* (tarnishing or whitewashing)—painting all employees in a work group with the same perceptional brush
2. *prejudice*—allowing good performance to be overshadowed by an employee's traits or qualities that the manager finds unattractive
3. *guilt by association*—employees are prejudged due to the company they keep
4. *dramatic incident effect*—one recent mistake or poor performance offsets the entire year's achievements
5. *difficult employee effect*—irritating, contrary, or opposite personality characteristics overshadow actual performance
6. *maverick effect*—the nonconformist may be downgraded because he or she is different
7. *weak team effect*—exemplary performance may be downplayed because the employee belongs to an underachieving work group

8. *unrealistic expectations effect*—expectations that are too high are brought about by the evaluator's perfectionism
9. *personality trait effect*—employees exhibit certain personality traits considered inappropriate
10. *self-comparison effect*—bias due to differentiation in the way a supervisor perceives a job should be carried out.

Other pitfalls or biases include *stereotyping, subjective performance standards, leniency,* and *opportunity biases.* Stereotyping involves basing developmental evaluations on fixed perceptions of performance rather than on actual accomplishments. Subjective performance standards allow employees and managers to hold different perceptions of performance outputs and activities. Some managers and supervisors give employees the benefit of the doubt when judging their performance. Consequently, they are guilty of leniency bias. Finally, opportunity bias occurs when the manager does not have adequate time to judge an employee's performance firsthand. Therefore, judgments are based on assumptions, central tendencies of a work group, or singular performance outputs or activities.

Effective managers not only recognize potential biases and pitfalls, but strive to eliminate them from employee performance judgments. This can best be accomplished by establishing specific, concise performance standards that are attached to performance outputs and activities. Performance standards provide employees with the type of information necessary for them to make performance judgments, and determine whether they are producing the kinds of results the organization desires. Managers benefit as performance standards provide the criteria necessary to conduct bias-free evaluations, neutralizing pitfalls and the halo and horn effects.

CONDUCTING DEVELOPMENTAL EVALUATIONS

Developmental evaluation interviews can be complex and time-consuming. To improve their efficiency and quality, a four-step process should be followed:

Step 1: Prepare for the developmental evaluation
Step 2: Conduct the developmental evaluation
Step 3: Assess the developmental evaluation
Step 4: Document results of the developmental evaluation

Step 1: Prepare for the Developmental Evaluation

Both managers and employees often perceive developmental evaluation interviews as confrontational, which is unfortunate. Hence the need to properly plan for such events. A poor interview can antagonize or demoralize a good employee, while a successful meeting can be exhilarating and motivating for both parties. To improve the outcome of these interviews, managers should decide the best time and place for the interview to take place—which is typically when and where both sides can spend quality time together without distraction, interruption, or interference.

An appropriate time should be scheduled well in advance so both parties' schedules can be coordinated. Immediately prior to a major project deadline, month-end report, or vacation are obviously not recommended. The setting should be a neutral, private room or office, off-site if necessary. Regardless, a location where manager and employee can be alone together without distractions remains crucial. We suggest an office without internal windows that would permit other employees or managers to observe the conversation. Absent sufficient privacy, employees may be reluctant to share their opinions openly and honestly. One of the author's former managers regularly treated interviewees to breakfast or lunch, preferring to conduct the evaluation at a quiet restaurant. The effect was overwhelmingly positive. This approach makes employees feel valued, strengthening positive feedback while fostering an air of "working together" to improve performance or manage deficiencies.

Prior to the interview, managers should properly prepare the facility to create an environment that encourages the free exchange of ideas and opinions. The environment should allow the manager and employee to function as equals in discussions via tactics such as placing chairs side by side and having beverages or snacks available. We highly discourage having the interviewer sit behind a desk as this demonstrates and reinforces his or her authority position over the employee.

Preparing for a developmental evaluation interview should also include gathering information and materials relevant to the discussion. While this may include appraisal or review forms provided by the organization, we will discuss later in this chapter how these forms impede the developmental process, discourage the free exchange of ideas, and violate the spirit of *developmental* evaluations. If these forms *are* used, they should be prepared along with appropriate supplemental information in support of the manager's position or perspective.

Another important aspect of preparation involves clearly communicating the type of developmental evaluation to be conducted. For example, a developmental planning interview differs greatly from a compensation review. As discussed previously, employees sometimes confuse the two and arrive at the meeting prepared only to review their annual increase or anticipated bonus. These two events should be separate reviews. Thus it remains critically important to communicate to the employee the type of review to be conducted, an overview of discussion topics, its purpose, and its focus. As a result, managers demonstrate respect for members of their team while employees have an opportunity to prepare accordingly.

Finally, managers should examine their strategies to create an environment conducive to the sharing of information and ideas. Good or bad, every meeting has an opening, body, and conclusion. Careful planning of the approach includes climate-setting comments designed to reduce stress for both parties along with a brief overview of the agenda. The heart of the meeting entails consideration of items to be discussed and the manner in which they will be handled. Planning the conclusion and follow-up activities guarantees closure for both parties while emphasizing continuous review and reinforcement of the agreed-on action plan.

Step 2: Conduct the Developmental Evaluation

Developmental evaluation interviews discuss performance, not personalities, in a future-oriented framework as opposed to a past-oriented one. While emphasis focuses on an employee's future actions instead of dwelling on past performance, the past *does* provide a means of sculpting and structuring the future. The following general guidelines will help prepare for the actual interview process, regardless of its type. These guidelines ensure establishment of an environment exuding respect for employees and their contributions during the term evaluated. They also serve as a reminder of the participatory emphasis of evaluation interviews, reinforcing their developmental nature. To ensure successful evaluation interviews, managers should:

- establish and maintain rapport with their employees
- explain clearly the interview's purpose
- encourage employees to share their opinions and ideas
- listen actively, without interruption, to employees' opinions and ideas

- avoid confrontation or arguments that lead to negative or destructive discourse
- focus on performance, not personalities
- focus on future, not past performance
- emphasize employee strengths as well as areas needing improvement
- terminate the interview on a positive note
- terminate the interview when all parties reach agreement (Kirkpatrick, 1985, pp. 55–57)

Five Steps of the Interview Process

The interviewing process begins by providing an overview of how the discussion will unfold, including steps to be followed during the meeting and the rules for engagement. Engagement rules include: two-way communication; open and honest dialogue; candor and substantive discussions based on actual performance supported by documentation. Once an overview has been provided, developmental evaluations entail five steps:

Interviewing Step 1: the employee shares his or her perspective and assessment of past performance,

Interviewing Step 2: the manager shares his or her assessment and identifies strengths, weaknesses, and areas requiring improvement,

Interviewing Step 3: the manager and employee compare assessments, identifying similarities and differences,

Interviewing Step 4: manager and employee develop an action plan for meeting goals, including changes in performance as well as growth and development planning activities, and

Interviewing Step 5: manager and employee establish progress review activities.

Interviewing Step 1: Employee Shares His or Her Perspective— The most logical step in conducting developmental evaluations is to allow the employee to conduct a performance self-appraisal since his or her last review. Self-appraisal is appropriate for all five types of evaluation review and necessary to establish employee opinions as a baseline for discussion. It also serves as a way of comparing manager/ employee perceptions and assessment in order to identify areas of agreement and disagreement. When seeking an employee's opinion of his or her performance, a manager may be able to minimize the amount of disagreement or confrontation that sometimes accompanies evaluations. The following examples may be useful in soliciting employee opinions: "Please share with me your opinion of your overall performance since your last review." "Where do you think you are doing well, and in which areas do you feel you need improvement?" An effective manager carefully listens to the employee's self-appraisal, encouraging him or her to begin with the year's achievements before moving to areas requiring improvement. It is extremely important that he or she be given an opportunity to identify and reinforce performance strengths rather than dwell on weaknesses.

Interviewing Step 2: Manager Shares His or Her Assessment— After an employee has shared his or her opinion of performance since the last review, the manager provides assessment of overall performance. This is the heart of the developmental evaluation process. Managers are responsible for discussing specific strengths and weaknesses of performance and how such conclusions were derived. They should be willing to share specific documentation, work samples, or other data that support or reinforce their point of view. Sharing of this information demonstrates thoughtfulness of evaluation and analysis of performance, and shows that perceptions are based on concrete facts rather than arbitrary whims or generalizations. Further, feedback is provided on job proficiencies and strengths as well as observations of how performance outputs and activities compare with standards.

Managers must be honest in evaluation, openly discussing performance areas needing improvement. Sugarcoating the truth helps no one, but it does position the employee for disaster later. Opinions and concerns expressed during formal evaluations may tremendously impact the employee's long-term performance capabilities. Whenever possible, managers should offer reassurance, maintaining a positive developmental approach when sharing the assessment. At all times they should avoid negative attacks on the employee's performance or personality. Instead of responding to negative statements of any kind, feelings should be rephrased or summarized to avoid defensive reactions.

Interviewing Step 3: Manager and Employee Compare Assessments— Next, managers and employees compare their respective assessments. The purpose of sharing assessments is for managers and employees to work collaboratively together toward the identification of areas of agreement and disagreement between their respective assessments of employee performance, strengths, weaknesses, and areas of improvement. It is important to focus on areas of disagreement in all categories, discussing each thoroughly. The purpose of this discussion is to reach consensus or resolution of differences. As managers and employees share perspectives on key performance areas, four possible responses may surface:

1. managers can revise their perspectives and areas of disagreement
2. employees can revise their perspectives and areas of disagreement
3. managers and employees can collaboratively compromise on differences by finding middle ground
4. managers and employees can agree to disagree amiably with the proviso that during the following year they will continue to document their respective differences toward resolution

If performance has not been satisfactory (which should not come as a surprise to employees), managers should focus on one or two critical areas where improvement is needed. Although total agreement may not be possible, an understanding should be reached of each other's views. An effective manager offers specific feedback on how to improve and asks for suggestions. The goal is for the employee to take responsibility for his or her actions and to correct deficiencies.

Interviewing Step 4: Manager and Employee Develop an Action Plan for Meeting Employee's Performance Goals—The fundamental purpose of a developmental evaluation is to identify ways of improving employee performance. In order to do so, it is essential to create an action plan that allows employees to maximize strengths, minimize weaknesses, and overcome deficiencies. In Chapter 7, we will discuss in detail how managers and employees can create performance growth and development plans designed to enhance performance. This formal step in the performance management process is enhanced via an action plan that serves as an antecedent to such an activity. That is, it's important during developmental evaluation interviews to discuss how employees plan to improve their performance. In some respects, this discussion is simply the process of establishing the parameters, conditions, and specifications required when developing a formal growth and development plan. Questions to consider include the following:

- What are the stated or understood performance goals for the future?
- What steps can the employee take to build on identified strengths?
- What specific steps must be taken to improve performance?
- How much improvement is needed, and by when?
- How can managers assist employees in the creation of formal growth and development plans?

The best action plans are those the employee develops for himself or herself. Moreover, employees are more likely to support the decisions or initiatives for which they've had input.

Interviewing Step 5: Manager and Employee Establish Progress Review Activities—At the conclusion of a developmental evaluation interview managers should summarize the main points discussed with employees, reviewing the strengths, weaknesses, and areas of improvement document collaboratively created along with the action plan employees intend to initiate. As with any important undertaking, feedback and follow-up are critical; thus managers and employees should discuss the importance of periodic progress reviews to emphasize the expected execution of a growth and development plan. Scheduling progress reviews at this time provides convenient, mutually agreed-on dates for further discussions. Further, managers demonstrate their commitment to helping the employee improve his or her performance by reviewing progress or examining any problems regularly. Progress reviews are necessary to ensure adequate performance improvement and employee commitment to their own growth and development.

Step 3: Assess the Developmental Evaluation

Completion of a developmental evaluation interview requires manager evaluation to determine its effectiveness as well as areas needing improvement. One effective means is to consider several important questions. Did the interview achieve its purpose? Did I help the employee examine his or her performance? How could I have made the interview more productive? What changes could I have made in my approach to achieve a better outcome? What items or subjects could I have discussed that were omitted? What unnecessary items could I have omitted from the discussion? What did I learn about my own skills and abilities? What did I learn about my employee that I didn't know before? Am I satisfied with the interview? Do we (manager and employee) have a better understanding of each other as a result of the interview? Do I feel that I am able to conduct my next interview more effectively? What did I learn about my interviewing techniques (i.e., questioning, listening, handling difficulties)?

Each of these questions provides managers with an opportunity to reflect on the interviewing process, its outcomes, and the employer–employee relationship that has been enhanced as a result. As with their employees, managers should identify their own strengths, weaknesses, and areas requiring improvement to create their own growth and development plan designed to improve their evaluation interviewing skills.

Step 4: Document Results of the Developmental Evaluation

Regardless of the type of review being conducted, documentation of employer–employee discussions is critical. This is done in order to comply with legal requirements and specific federal and state laws governing employee practices. In essence, leave a paper trail—our litigious society demands it.

Formal documentation can be used to evaluate, promote, reward, discipline, or terminate an employee; therefore, it is an extremely critical record. Documentation can also be used as a resource when conducting future developmental evaluations.

Formal documentation consists of performance information, developmental evaluation forms, previous compensation reviews, and timekeeping records. A complete record of discussions regarding consequences of continued poor performance should be documented in written form, including identification of any potential disciplinary action such as demotions or penalties.

While developmental evaluations are designed to help employees improve their performance, they are also used to determine future employment opportunities. In order to ensure that developmental evaluations are reasonable and defensible, they should be based on performance standards that are *known* to employees in advance (e.g., written and distributed to employees). Performance standards should be established for each and every performance output and activity an employee is responsible for completing. Performance standards should be specific, realistic, clear, concise, and written in such a way that employees can conduct their own performance evaluations. Employees should be given regular performance feedback from their managers and supervisors with supportive documentation identifying any performance problem or difficulty. Additionally, developmental evaluations should record all training and development activities made available to an employee. Finally, employees should have an opportunity to comment on their evaluations and share perspectives of their own performance.

DEALING WITH EMPLOYEE DISAGREEMENTS, EXCUSES, AND PERFORMANCE BARRIERS

When managers and employees discuss their differences, the conversation should be friendly, open, honest, and respectful. Developmental evaluations are designed to enhance performance, not place blame or accuse employees of wrongful acts. Occasionally, disagreements become

difficult to manage. At times, employees offer excuses for poor performance, feel that a performance problem is not important, want to discuss
irrelevant issues, fail to participate during the interview, want unavail-
able or unjustified promotions, or desire groundless merit increases.
When such difficulties surface, it is important to have a strategy for
dealing with them. We'll examine each troublesome situation separately
and provide recommendations for dealing with employees under each.

Manager and Employee Disagree on the Assessment

In this situation, both parties appear to be at an impasse. Managers
should initiate the following steps to reach agreement:

- demonstrate understanding of the employee's point of view
- be flexible (willing to change your mind)
- provide evidence to support your position or point of view
- check for agreement
- allow the employee the opportunity to reverse his or her position
  without losing face

If the employee continues to disagree, managers should request that he
or she express the disagreement in writing and provide suggestions for
correcting the performance problem.

Employee Offers Excuses for Poor Performance

In this circumstance, managers should consider the following suggestions:

- demonstrate understanding of the employee's view
- confirm that you have agreement that results are not satisfactory
- ask the employee what he or she could have done about the prob-
  lem(s)
- ask for solutions to correct the performance problem

Employee Believes That a Performance Problem Is not Important

Consider the following to counteract this situation:

- demonstrate understanding of the employee's view
- confirm that you have agreement on what has happened
- ask the employee about impacts of the performance problem

- check for agreement
- ask for suggestions for correcting the performance problem

Employee Wants to Discuss Irrelevant Issues

Overcoming this situation requires the following:

- recommend another, more appropriate time to discuss the issues
- demonstrate understanding of the employee's need to discuss such issues, but point out that the review's purpose is to . . .
- refocus the employee on the subject by asking specific questions pertaining to his or her exact performance

Employee Fails to Participate During the Interview

Lack of employee participation may be due to any number of factors, from shyness to stress to intimidation. When this occurs, managers should:

- reestablish rapport
- make certain they are not sharing too much information or dominating the conversation
- ask open-ended questions, pause, and absorb responses
- rephrase employee responses and ask for agreement
- minimize criticism or disagreements
- stress the importance of the employee's perspective
- indicate the value of the employee's perspective
- encourage the employee's full participation and cooperation

Employee Wants Unavailable or Unjustified Promotions

To overcome this phenomenon, managers should:

- support the employee's enthusiasm
- clarify organizational realities
- discuss requirements and responsibilities
- ask employees to review their knowledge, skills, and abilities vis-à-vis job responsibilities and requirements
- ask and comment on employee qualifications
- help employees formulate a plan to meet requirements
- advise that there are no guarantees that a promotion is imminent

Employee Wants to Discuss Unjustified Merit Increases

Many employees erroneously believe that their (poor) performance justifies an increase in compensation and that they have performed at an exemplary level. Others feel deserving of merit increases simply due to tenure. Under these circumstances, managers should discuss pay for performance plans or compensation policies that exist within the organization. They should compare an employee's actual performance with performance standards established for the job. Further, managers should clarify the organization's position regarding merit increases, addressing whether the employee has met or exceeded the standards necessary to receive such an increase.

Performance Barriers

Obstacles or barriers to performance take many shapes, both organizationally and employee-based. Whether these barriers originated in personal or family problems, job tasks, or the organizational environment, it is absolutely essential for managers and employees to review the obstacles that might prevent performance at an acceptable level. This discussion should focus on two levels. First, considerable time should be devoted to identifying and isolating obstacles. Second, means of neutralizing, eliminating, or managing barriers require evaluation to guarantee employees ample opportunity to perform at or above established standards.

Performance interference can be as simple as having inadequate resources to complete a job or as complicated as having competing tasks that prevent the job's timely execution. Regardless, obstacles and barriers must be identified and overcome, particularly when they prevent superior employees from performing at an adequate level.

THE EVALUATION FORM—A RESTRICTIVE DOCUMENT

Most organizations use performance appraisal or review forms to conduct employee appraisals. While these forms come in every shape and size, they have one common characteristic: the goal of making the performance review process as simple as possible. Organizations have attempted to make the performance appraisal (developmental evaluation) process a painless activity, encouraging managers and supervisors to assign a "number" for employees in every possible category.

Some organizations have gone to the expense of computer-generating performance appraisal forms to attain uniformity throughout their organizations. It is our belief that such forms are far more damaging than beneficial. It makes more sense for a manager to start with a blank sheet of paper on which he or she pens a developmental evaluation (with identified performance standards for all important categories) than to waste time filling out a performance appraisal form that has little or no value as a developmental tool. Few if any performance problems have been resolved through the use of such forms, which serve only as a mechanism by which to defend organizations during litigation. They do not serve as a developmental tool; consequently, we believe that such forms should not be used to conduct developmental evaluations.

If an organization lacks the time, energy, or dedication necessary to use the appraisal process in a constructive, developmental manner, it ceases to be of value. We understand organizations' needs to defend themselves from employees who feel as though they have been improperly treated. However, doesn't it make more sense to have comprehensive documentation of an employee's performance—and the manager's attempt to help an employee correct performance—than a simple 1–5 evaluation form? Isn't it more important to have documented work samples and observable evaluation data than a simple, scale appraisal form? After all, the purpose of this process is to help people grow and develop. If done in a constructive, helpful manner, most if not all employees will improve and enhance their performance.

Certainly, there are occasions when an employee has been improperly selected for a job, or his or her skills and knowledge have been mismatched to job activities or performance outputs required. This has little or nothing to do with developmental evaluations but rather is a recruiting and selection dilemma that may need to be addressed within the organization. We strongly urge organizations to eliminate use of such forms that provide weak support of one's legal position. Instead, turn performance appraisals into developmental evaluations designed to enhance employee growth and development.

CONCLUSION

Developmental evaluations are formalized feedback activities designed to provide employees with valuable information regarding the quantity and quality of their performance. To this end, developmental evaluations help organizations make difficult decisions regarding their employees' futures; they are useful in conducting work planning and review activities, compensation reviews, career planning, and human resource planning. They provide a forum in which employees create growth and development plans to overcome performance deficiencies while building on strengths and managing weaknesses.

The developmental evaluation portion of the performance alignment process helps employees when they:

- think there is a better way of doing their jobs (reason 11)
- are not confronted for performing their jobs incorrectly (reason 12)
- refuse to produce the performance outputs required (reason 13)
- think they are doing their jobs correctly (reason 14)
- have personal problems that prevent them from doing their jobs (reason 15, see Figure 1.3)

This phase also helps organizations address managerial malpractice (reason 4, see Figure 1.2).

Developmental evaluations and performance coaching activities are feedback processes that help organizations transform their employees into their greatest assets. As a result, these formal and informal feedback approaches enable employees to construct and develop strategies for their ongoing, continuous improvement that ultimately realize improved efficiency, profitability, and competitiveness for the organization.

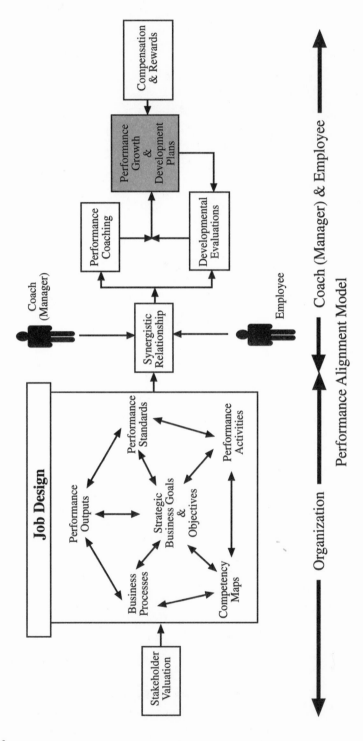

Chapter 7

CREATING PERFORMANCE GROWTH AND DEVELOPMENT PLANS

The primary purpose of developmental evaluations is for managers and employees to discuss ways of enhancing performance results. These conversations include an examination of employees' strengths, weaknesses, and areas for improvement. They become the focus of employee growth and development plans and should be perceived as a long-term developmental strategy instead of a quick fix.

Managers and employees should mutually design growth and development plans, which should be realistic, specific, attainable, and tied to a timetable. Delaying implementation of a growth and development plan may diminish its effectiveness, importance, and value; therefore it it should be initiated immediately. Delays may also give managers who are not truly interested in their employees' growth and development the opportunity to procrastinate.

Employees engage in the design and construction of performance growth and development plans by identifying developmental and performance objectives, specifying learning sources and strategies they will use to acquire new skills and knowledge, identifying transfer of learning strategies that promote application of new learning to the job, identifying project completion target dates, and assisting in the measurement of learning acquisition and transfer on the job. Manager participation includes providing employees with performance feedback and reinforcement, conducting performance measurement activities, and examining learning acquisition during future developmental evaluation reviews.

FORGING A PERFORMANCE GROWTH AND DEVELOPMENT PARTNERSHIP

Managers and employees should work closely together in the creation of a performance growth and development plan. This requires them to create a partnership focused on acquiring new learning and applying it to the job. A mutually beneficial performance growth and development partnership allows employees to acquire critical skills and competencies used to enhance their performance and career development opportunities (reason 8, see Figure 1.3). In this way, managers solicit the involvement and support of employees in their growth and development, which addresses one of the primary reasons organizations fail to achieve desired performance results (reason 6, see Figure 1.2). Moreover, managers will enjoy better business results when employees willingly participate in growth and development plans that enable them to meet departmental goals and objectives.

The success of growth and development partnerships depends on five requirements. First, employees must *want* to change their performance behavior. That is, they must have the desire to acquire new knowledge and skills or build on existing ones. They must also be dedicated to transferring new learning to their jobs.

Second, performance growth and development plans must be based on identifying employees' performance improvement needs, determining the barriers that prevent learning acquisition and transfer, addressing cultural issues that reduce employee motivation, identifying conflicting job tasks and activities that diminish learning, and providing performance feedback and reinforcement on the job. These activities are primarily the responsibility of managers during this partnership.

When these activities are applied correctly, managers create cooperative learning environments that are conducive to employee growth and development. Such environments amplify learning opportunities by providing employees with a secure, comfortable atmosphere that encourages them to apply new knowledge and skills. These learning environments encourage employee transfer of new knowledge and skills to the job and hold them accountable for its acquisition.

Managers foster an appropriate learning environment by encouraging employees to participate in learning acquisition and transfer activities. They should resist the temptation to tell employees what they need to know and how they need to learn it. Managers must, however, guard against remaining too neutral, allowing employees to acquire unnecessary or irrelevant knowledge and skills. Instead, they should be active participants in knowledge inquiry and transfer. Managers should avoid making negative statements that discourage employees from changing their behaviors. They should not put restrictions on learning acquisition strategies unless these are in serious violation of organizational policies or procedures, or are too costly. Sharing, supportive environments demonstrate managers' deep concern for the well-being of their employees. Once established, supportive environments encourage employees to advance their skills and enhance their performance.

Third, employees share in these partnerships by realizing that they are ultimately responsible for acquiring learning and transferring it to the job. Moreover, employees must identify the knowledge and skills they desire to change. They must also have the desire and ability to manage their own learning and work environments in order to create conditions where learning transfer flourishes. This type of self-discipline is not present in all employees, which is one of the reasons learning transfer does not occur in every situation. The success of performance growth and development partnerships depends on the employee's aptitude for acquiring new knowledge and skills, self-control and discipline, high achievement needs, and motivation to use new skills on the job.

Fourth, if employees are to improve their performance they will need encouragement and assistance from their managers. Occasionally, employees are afraid to participate in developmental activities because they fear failure. Some employees lack the confidence to participate without encouragement or assistance, while others possess every intention of participating, but are either too disorganized to start or fall victim to procrastination.

Fifth, many employees fail to participate in growth and development plans because they are not rewarded for their efforts. While seemingly shortsighted, many are convinced that unless the organization is willing to provide monetary compensation, changing their performance behaviors is unnecessary (see Chapter 8).

When each of these five requirements for behavioral change is satisfied, most employees will be willing to participate in organized growth and development plans. Managers should make certain that employees know exactly what behavioral changes are expected, which skills need improvement, and what level of performance is required. Managers must also make certain that learning acquisition can occur on or through the job, and that employees will be given adequate support and encouragement as they attempt to integrate new knowledge and skills.

MOTIVATING EMPLOYEES

Managers who want their employees to participate in performance growth and development plans need to recognize that employees have reasons for everything they do. Managers should realize that employees choose to perform the way they do because of some internal or external motivation. Employees decide to change those things that they perceive aren't good for them. In other words, employees choose to change their performance behaviors because they see some kind of immediate or long-term payoff. Employees participate when the goal they have chosen to pursue is attainable. To ensure greater participation, managers must understand this simple motivational principle.

Carlisle and Murphy (1996) believe that employee motivation can be greatly enhanced when managers understand the seven assumptions that underlie change behavior. First, employees are motivated to change their behavior when given clear, sharply focused objectives. Employees are not encouraged to participate in change activities when they are written in ambiguous, unmeasurable terms. Examples such as "Do a better job" or "Try harder" are both ambiguous and nonquantifiable. Consequently, employees will avoid such requests. Managers who help identify skill gaps and work closely with their employees in the construction of performance objectives that are clear and precise have a much better opportunity to enhance employee growth and development.

Second, employees need to thoroughly understand how to perform their jobs correctly. Employees need to know not only what to do but also how to accomplish the task. Any attempt to motivate an employee to change without adhering to this basic assumption may be counterproductive. Most employees want to perform their jobs correctly. Failing to tell them exactly what to do and how to do it will serve as a demotivator.

Third, employees are more likely to change their performance behaviors when they are given opportunities to participate in problem-solving and decision-making activities that directly affect them. Employees need to be given the authority to make decisions about how to improve their performance.

Fourth, change requires personal commitment for action, which obligates managers to secure employee buy-in prior to the creation of growth and development plans. In this way, employees own the learning acquisition and transfer process.

Fifth, managers must clearly communicate positive and negative rewards that are linked directly to performance improvement. Care must be taken when identifying rewards to ensure that correct behavior is rewarded rather than punished; rewards for poor performance must be eliminated. Too often, managers fail to confront employees when they have not performed adequately—inadvertently rewarding undesirable behaviors or performance. As a result, employees may experience confusion or lack of motivation.

Sixth, managers must demonstrate patient, persistent follow-through when providing positive feedback and reinforcement. Receiving performance feedback and reinforcement is similar to receiving a much-needed drink of water after traversing an arid desert. It both refreshes and renews one's commitment, vitality, and enthusiasm to continue.

Seventh, managers need to be realistic regarding the types of rewards offered, while acting within their discretion and authority. It is counterproductive to *offer* promotions, merit pay, bonuses, or other material rewards if they cannot be granted to employees. False hopes or expectations lead to distrust and the deterioration of synergistic relationships. Carlisle and Murphy (1996) further add that performance change requires skilled managers who can organize and prepare a motivating environment, communicate with motivating presentations, handle employees' questions, generate creative ideas, prioritize ideas, direct employees' practices, plan employees' actions, commit employees to action, and provide follow-up that overcomes motivational problems (p. 186). When organizations make it a practice to recruit, hire, and select skilled managers such as these, they are well on the way to addressing the performance challenge.

CREATING A SELF-ESTEEMING ENVIRONMENT

Managers interact with their employees every day, which provides them numerous opportunities to enhance or diminish employee self-esteem. These interactions may include delegating or observing work assignments or activities, one-on-one meetings, performance confrontations, discussions, presentations, proposals, and so on. Together, these interactions comprise employees' "private and public world," a world they draw on to bolster their self-esteem. On the other hand, this world can deplete self-esteem, particularly when negative interactions result in feelings of depression, anger, or resentment.

Over time, employees' interactions comprise a "net balance" of experiences—both positive and negative. For some, this produces a positive self-concept that enables them to feel comfortable with themselves, giving them the confidence to take risks, grow, and be unique or expressive, courageous, or self-assured. Employees with a positive self-concept are able to be and become whatever they desire. Conversely, employees possessing a negative self-concept are often defensive, frightened, mistrusting, reclusive, critical, bitter, or resentful. When these attitudes prevail, employees are reluctant to take on new challenges or be receptive to advice or constructive criticism. Their attitude toward growth and development activities is often negative, as these actions are perceived as additional work instead of a challenge or growth opportunity. Consequently, these employees find fault with the organization, its managers, or their co-workers.

Gilley and Boughton (1996) believe that the primary purpose of the performance coaching and developmental evaluation process is to enhance the self-esteem of employees. They refer to this process as "self-esteeming" (p. 188), which they define as the complementary synergistic relationship between managers and employees—a relationship where the whole is greater than the sum of the parts. This relationship is based on the enormously powerful need of managers and employees to feel good about themselves and their experiences, skills, and abilities. In short, self-esteeming is the sum total of how managers and employees feel about themselves.

Self-esteeming is a bit like a debit and credit account from which employees draw to build up or tear down their self-concepts. The balance within the account fluctuates based on interactions within their environment (i.e., their experiences). Therefore, self-esteeming is the net of an employee's experiences, which forms a positive or negative self-concept.

Managers possess the critically important responsibility of improving the self-esteem of their employees as each and every interaction enhances or depletes an employee's self-concept. Therefore, employee work assignments (i.e., interactions) can energize and keep employees engaged or diminish their self-concepts. Interactions help employees grow and develop, which encourages them to tackle increasingly difficult, challenging assignments, or these interactions can foster dependency and self-doubt.

Perhaps one of the major obstacles in addressing the performance challenge is identifying ways of enhancing employees' self-esteem. While stakeholder evaluation, job design, synergistic relationships, performance coaching, and developmental evaluations are critical to addressing the performance challenge, these will be piecemeal events unless means are discovered of enhancing employees' overall self-concept. The only way to truly integrate the components of the performance alignment process is to discover and implement means by which to grow and develop employees.

Four primary sources contribute to enhancing an employee's self-esteem. They are:

- achievement, accomplishment, and mastery
- power, control, and influence
- being cared about and valued
- acting on values and beliefs (Bradshaw, 1981, p. 23)

Each of these sources serves as a conduit through which employees' experiences (world) can influence their overall self-esteem level. These four sources of self-esteem enable positive experiences to flow into the employee's self-concept bucket. The more positive experiences employees have, the higher their self-esteem level will become. The higher their self-esteem level, the greater their self-concept will be.

Over time, employees' experiences either add to or subtract from their self-concept buckets, which either raises or lowers their level of self-esteem. When employees experience negative interactions, they will need to find activities that replenish their self-esteem level. The net effect is a lower self-concept, producing negative employees and poor outcomes. Employees cannot engage in positive interactions if they can't rebuild their self-esteem. If this cycle is allowed to continue, the result is angry, resentful employees who are fearful of management and the organization. These employees avoid taking risks, making recommendations for improvement, or engaging in professional growth and development opportunities. Consequently, managers must find ways to fill their employees' self-concept buckets. This can best be done by using one or all of the aforementioned four sources of self-esteem.

Achievement, Accomplishment, and Mastery

Every employee needs opportunities to achieve or accomplish something meaningful. This may include acquiring new skills or knowledge, participating in creative endeavors, being granted new and exciting responsibilities, participating in visible, important projects, or providing opinions and insights regarding the organization's direction. The possibilities are endless. Whether the manager perceives the experience as positive remains irrelevant. Whether the employee benefits from the experience and his or her self-esteem rises is the critical issue.

Once an employee has identified a project or activity that has the potential to help improve his or her self-esteem, managers have the responsibility to provide regular, timely feedback regarding performance. It is not enough for employees to engage in activities that have the potential to improve their self-esteem; they must also receive the kind of reinforcement that gives them confidence and reassurance—which can only come from their managers or supervisors. Little satisfaction or self-esteem growth occurs unless employees receive performance feedback on a regular basis and immediately after results have been achieved.

Power, Control, and Influence

Providing employees with opportunities to have influence over decisions, authority over others, and power and control greatly enhances their self-esteem. Many employees identify with the traditional symbols of success such as job titles, increased office space, and access to key decision makers. Furthermore, they want the organization to provide these opportunities as well as reward and recognize their contributions.

Managers can greatly increase employees' self-esteem by doing a number of simple activities that cost the organization little. These things include appointing employees to be members of decision-making committees, task forces, or teams that have influence over their part of organizational life. Other activities may be as simple as asking employees' opinions regarding upcoming changes or suggestions for improving organizational efficiency and effectiveness. Too many organizations fail to solicit or include employees' input and support regarding organizational change. Employee involvement and participation, when discounted, diminishes their self-worth, undercuts their effectiveness, and degrades them as human beings, rendering them powerless. Is it any wonder that organizational announcements regarding major changes are met with employee hostility or resentment? Nothing is more demeaning or a source of anger and frustration than having an important or significant event occur for which an employee has had no input, influence, or control. Consequently, loss of power over decision making results in lost respect on the part of employees.

Being Cared About and Valued

Many employees go to work every day of the week, hoping they will receive some type of positive affirmation for their existence. Unfortunately, many managers discount the importance of a positive relationship, regarding it as unnecessary or insignificant. For many employees, personal involvement is an essential source of self-esteem, and managers should act on this fact accordingly. It does not cost an organization a single penny to treat employees with dignity and respect—the kind of positive regard that is afforded people of significance (such as the president, CEO, major stockholders, or customers). Simple acknowledgment of employees' contributions, recommendations, or achievements goes a long way toward improving their self-esteem.

Acting on Values and Beliefs

At the heart of every employee's behavior is a set of values and beliefs that guide their actions. These values and beliefs serve as a source of positive self-esteem if employees are able to act consistently on them. However, the reverse is also true. When circumstances prevent employees from acting on their values and beliefs, they can become resentful, angry, or depressed. These emotions produce negative self-esteem.

When employees are allowed to behave in accordance with their basic values and beliefs, they feel good about themselves and their overall self-esteem improves. Being allowed to make decisions that are based on one's values and beliefs is a freeing experience that enables employees to feel as though they have control over their own lives and those things that are important to them. Allowing employees to act on their values and beliefs is sometimes difficult for authoritative, controlling managers. They must relinquish decision making to their employees, allowing them to make decisions that are consistent with their internal core values and beliefs.

When employees are allowed to draw on one or more of the four sources of self-esteem, their self-concept improves. They feel more competent and energized, resulting in greater organizational commitment, risk taking, openness, cooperation, courage, candor, creativity, and growth. Conversely, the opposite is also true. Employees who are not allowed to participate in interactions that improve their self-esteem are made to feel inadequate, resulting in lower trust, anger, suspicion, low risk taking, stagnation, and low creativity. Consequently, poor performance and low quality are indicative of employees who possess negative self-concepts. It is, therefore, the responsibility of every manager within the organization to find ways of bolstering employees' self-esteem.

DELEGATION AS A GROWTH AND DEVELOPMENT STRATEGY

An often-overlooked performance growth and development strategy is that of delegating work assignments to employees to improve their skills and abilities. Gilley (1998) defines delegation as appointing someone to operate on your behalf. In other words, delegation implies that employees are interchangeable parts used to produce desired results, serving as replacements for other employees, assuming their tasks and responsibilities.

Many managers fear delegating work to employees, often contending that it takes twice as long to explain how to do a job task as it would to do it themselves. Some managers believe that employees will "screw it up," while others assert, "I don't think they can do it as well as I can." These weak excuses prevent employees from growing and developing. Managers must remember that their job is to secure results through people. Therefore, they must learn to delegate tasks and responsibilities in order to achieve desired organizational results.

While delegation is an everyday event in most organizations, it is seldom seen as a growth and development strategy. The primary reason delegation is successful is that it allows more experienced managers and employees to delegate tasks and responsibilities to less-experienced employees, giving them the opportunity to acquire new knowledge, skills, and competencies. Over time, the delegation cycle enhances an individual's performance capacity to such a point that he or she is able to take on even more difficult tasks and responsibilities. As the cycle continues, employees grow and develop, enabling them to become more important assets within the organization. Consequently, delegation is quintessentially a growth and development strategy.

Delegation involves four basic activities:

1. identifying responsibilities and tasks to be delegated
2. granting appropriate levels of authority
3. identifying and eliminating performance barriers
4. discussing and defining accountability

The first step in the delegation cycle involves identifying tasks and responsibilities to be delegated, which often requires managers to analyze jobs, determine which tasks are most appropriate for delegation, and clarify the expected results. Once specified, managers should meet with their employees to explain their work assignment rationale and allow employees to ask questions or share opinions.

Second, managers should outline the level of authority being granted to their employees. This answers the question, "What authority can the employee exercise to accomplish the task at hand?" The authority granted in a delegation depends on the employee's experience and the manager's confidence in her or his skills and abilities. Experience is based on the performance history of the employee, while confidence refers to the extent to which the manager trusts the employee's abilities. The combination of confidence and experience determines the level of authority granted. Placing confidence on a vertical axis (low–moderate–high) and experience on a horizontal axis (limited–extensive), a working model forms that demonstrates five levels of authority. They are placed according to an employee's level of experience (1–9) and the confidence others have in his or her abilities (1–9). The levels of authority are represented by:

- rookie (1,1)—limited experience, low confidence
- worker bee (5,5)—moderate experience, moderate confidence
- new member (9,1)—extensive experience, low confidence
- rising star (1,9)—limited experience, high confidence
- partner (9,9)—extensive experience, high confidence (Figure 7.1)

When considering delegating tasks and responsibilities to an employee, it is important to identify the appropriate level of authority. Employee experience and the manager's confidence in their skills and abilities determines which level of authority is granted. For example:

Rookie (1,1) At this level of authority, experience is limited and confidence is low. The employee gets the facts (i.e., gathers data,

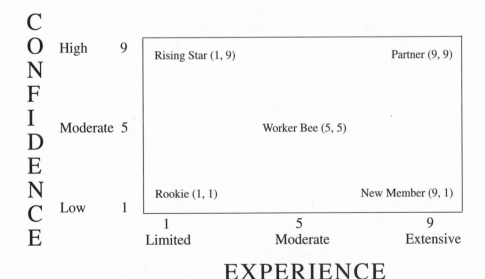

Figure 7.1 Five Levels of Authority

prepares data requests), but the manager decides what further actions are necessary. As the employee successfully completes assignments, the manager's confidence rises.

Worker Bee (5,5) Here, experience and confidence are both moderate. The employee decides the actions to be taken, but the manager maintains veto power. This limits the employee's freedom until he or she has gained even more experience and the manager's confidence rises higher. Performance feedback and monitoring activities are still very important at this stage.

New Member (9,1) This employee's experience is extensive, but the manager has little or no firsthand knowledge of his or her performance, hence, little confidence. Managers let this type of employee handle the task, but closely monitor performance. Feedback is not as critical here because the employee has performed successfully in the past. Monitoring future performance is the best way of increasing the manager's confidence in the employee's skills and abilities.

Rising Star (1,9) At this level, experience is limited although the manager has complete confidence in the "potential abilities" of the employee. Under this condition, the manager works closely with the employee by training him or her and assigning tasks to be completed, providing positive and constructive feedback about performance. Serving as a mentor (performance coaching role) is most appropriate when working with this type of employee.

Partner (9,9) At this point, experience is extensive and confidence is high. The employee is free to act and simply report results. Here the employee is operating on the manager's behalf, at the highest level of authority (Gilley & Marquart, 1994).

Once the most appropriate level of authority to be granted to the employee has been identified, a few moments should be spent with the employee discussing possible performance barriers. Collaborative identification of ways in which performance barriers can be eliminated or overcome strengthens the synergistic relationship, and gives the employee an opportunity to discuss more thoroughly the exact performance outputs expected.

Delegation activity is simply assigning an employee a task or responsibility that is otherwise part of someone else's job. Consequently, when a manager delegates a work assignment to an employee, the manager remains accountable for the delegation's outcome. That is, tasks and responsibilities may be delegated, but accountability cannot. Accountability rests with the individual who was originally assigned the task or responsibility. Therefore, it is important to have an open, honest discussion about the accountability relationship that occurs as a result of the delegation. In this way, employees know exactly what they're accountable for, and to whom they are accountable. When delegation occurs, employees become accountable to the manager for completing the task or responsibility, while the manager is held ultimately accountable to his or her boss.

To improve delegation skills, the following guidelines are offered for consideration:

1. *decide what to delegate*—who is qualified, and what support or training they need
2. *plan the delegation*—review all essential details and decisions, determine appropriate feedback controls, provide for training and coaching, and establish performance standards
3. *select the right person*—consider employees' interests, skills, abilities, and their qualifications to complete the assignment
4. *delegate effectively*—clarify the results expected and priorities involved, specify level of authority granted, and identify importance of the assignment, feedback, and reporting requirements
5. *follow up*—insist on results but not perfection, demand timely performance reports, encourage independence, don't short-circuit or take back the assignment, and reward good performance (Gilley and Boughton, 1996, p. 25)

BUILDING ON STRENGTHS AND MANAGING WEAKNESSES

There is an assumption that fixing employees' weaknesses will improve their performance and enhance organizational effectiveness. In fact, all training activities are based on this premise. Sadly, this assumption is false. According to Clifton and Nelson (1992), fixing employees' weaknesses only makes their performance normal or average, not outstanding. They believe that excellence can only be achieved by building on employees' strengths and managing their weaknesses, not via the elimination of their weaknesses.

Because most training activities focus on fixing weaknesses, managers have the misguided perception that their job is to identify and isolate their employees' weaknesses. Consequently, they use traditional performance appraisals to amass evidence that supports this belief.

Unfortunately, this is one of the biggest mistakes managers make. We believe it would be much more effective to design growth and development plans that enable employees to build on their strengths and areas of expertise while managing weaknesses.

Clifton and Nelson (1992) identify four characteristics to be used in determining employee strengths:

1. passionate interest in a particular activity or subject
2. high levels of personal satisfaction when performing a particular task or activity
3. rapid and continuous learning
4. achieving exceptional results when participating in a particular task or activity

Nothing is more important when fostering performance growth and development than shifting the focus from *fixing* weaknesses to *maximizing strengths and managing weaknesses*.

Identifying weaknesses is the first step in managing them. Weaknesses are easier to spot than strengths because we are conditioned to search for weaknesses. Weaknesses have been pointed out to employees most of their lives. Teachers, parents, previous supervisors, even spouses have been telling employees the things they don't do well. Certain identifying characteristics highlight employee weaknesses, including:

1. slow learning on the part of the employee
2. inability to remember simple steps and procedures of a task
3. defensiveness regarding performance
4. avoidance of particular tasks or activities

When managing weaknesses, identification is only the first step. Next comes development of strategies that help employees manage their weaknesses. Clifton and Nelson (1992) identify four strategies that managers can use to help their employees manage weaknesses. They include delegating, partnering, preventing, and alternatives.

Delegating is one of the best ways of managing employee weaknesses as it allows employees to work on tasks and activities that they are best suited for, rather than those at which they are unable to produce positive results.

Partnering is not that of the traditional sense—the matching of one person's strengths to another's weaknesses. Rather, it is a teaming that combines two employees' strengths together to achieve a goal. Employees' complementary strengths overcome many weaknesses they might possess. This strategy may need to be combined with delegating in order to guarantee that critical tasks are completed on time, within budget, and at the correct level of quality.

Some employees simply need to exercise their right of refusal to participate in certain tasks or activities in what is known as preventing. The primary difficulty in executing this strategy lies in managers' inability to be flexible when assigning work tasks and activities. It makes very little sense to assign an employee a task or activity which he or she is unable to complete successfully. It makes much more sense to give such a task or activity to an individual who possesses the talent or ability to achieve the desired results. While this may appear to be favoritism on the manager's part, in reality it utilizes a commonsense approach to performance management.

Finally, managers must be willing to accept different ways of accomplishing the same tasks. In other words, there may be several acceptable methods of successfully demonstrating a performance activity. Some of the best quality improvements and performance efficiencies have been discovered when managers encouraged their employees to find alternative ways to complete a job. Encouraging employees to use alternatives that build on their strengths enhances their self-esteem.

DESIGNING LEARNING ACQUISITION AND TRANSFER PLANS

One of the best ways for organizations to enhance employee growth and development is by facilitating learning acquisition and transfer. The learning acquisition and transfer process helps employees acquire the skills, abilities, and competencies needed to enhance their performance. In this way, the learning acquisition and transfer process produces specific outcomes on which organizations can rely to help them achieve their strategic business goals and objectives. The learning acquisition and transfer process also encourages employee involvement and is an essential element in developing a long-term strategy for performance growth and development (reason 6, see Figure 1.2).

The learning acquisition and transfer process consists of five steps that are mutually completed by managers and employees. They are:

1. identifying performance objectives
2. identifying learning resources and strategies
3. creating transfer of learning strategies

4. identifying target dates for completion of each performance objective
5. measuring performance enhancement and improvement (Figure 7.2)

Performance Objectives	Learning Resources	Transfer of Learning Strategies	Target Date	Measure of Performance

Figure 7.2 Learning Acquisition and Transfer Contract

First, employees identify performance objectives—what they will do differently on completion of their learning and acquisition plan. This activity translates the identified performance need(s) and desire(s) into performance objectives that are written to describe what the employee will do differently on the job as a result of learning. Performance objectives differ from learning objectives in that they describe in detail the types of performance employees wish to demonstrate rather than what they desire to learn. Employees should write a specific performance objective for each identified performance need or desire. Performance objectives may be written to acquire knowledge, skills, attitudes, values, understanding, or awareness—and should be written in such a way as to demonstrate a change in their performance. Once written, these objectives serve as the focus of remaining sections of the learning acquisition and transfer plan.

A well-written performance objective should (1) be clear and understandable, (2) identify what the employee will do as a result of acquiring new learning, (3) describe the observed behavior that will demonstrate that learning occurred, (4) identify the acceptable level of performance or the performance behavior, (5) describe conditions under which performance will be measured, and (6) be stated in such a way that the degree to which it is accomplished can be measured (Gilley & Maycunich, 1998).

Second, an employee should describe how performance objectives are to be achieved. When this has been accomplished, employees have identified the learning resources and strategies they intend to use in accomplishing their performance objectives. Learning resources and strategies can include both human and material resources such as books, journal articles, handouts, newspapers, lists of suggested readings, resource persons, peers, employees, supervisors, mentors, professional trainers, videotapes, cassettes, and so on. Strategies are the way the identified resources will be used, including going to the library or learning resource center, reading book chapters or articles, making observations, discussing best practices with colleagues, experts, or supervisors using structured questions and interviewing techniques, working on inquiry teams (a group of two or more people responsible for addressing specific questions about a topic or element of an issue and taking full responsibility for discovering the answers or solutions to them), and so forth. Several resources and strategies may be listed for each identified performance objective.

Third, learning acquisition must be transferred to the job in order for it to be of value to the organization. Therefore, learning transfer strategies must be identified to guarantee that employees use what they learn on the job. On the surface, learning transfer appears to be a simple, straightforward task, although a number of barriers constantly prevent it from occurring. Barriers include employees, managers, the organization, or human resource development (HRD) professionals. Employees fail to transfer learning to the job for many reasons, particularly because: there is no payoff for acquiring new skills or knowledge, new learning conflicts with their deeply held values and beliefs, they lack confidence in using new skills or applying new knowledge, they fear change and therefore extinguish any new learning that might be acquired as a result, or application on the job has been delayed resulting in de-learning.

Managers often prevent learning transfer when they fail to be positive role models for their employees, allowing employees to make excuses for not applying what they have learned. Sometimes, managers fail to control an employee's peers who are being critical of the acquisition of new knowledge, thereby creating an environment that is not conductive to learning transfer. The most serious violations on the part of managers include failure to coach employees, failure to provide positive reinforcement, and failure to provide performance standards by which employees can measure their new performance behaviors on the job. In order to overcome these failures, managers and employees must develop a performance improvement partnership that allows employees to increase their application and integration of learning—which will ultimately help the organization achieve better results (Figure 7.3).

Organizations also present barriers to learning transfer. Unless these barriers are eliminated, learning transfer is doomed to failure. The most common learning transfer barriers include an inappropriate incentive or reward system, maintaining poor management practices (i.e., allowing managerial malpractice to continue), providing negative consequences for learning transfer, and failing to eliminate task interference.

Many organizations still rely on HRD professionals to provide training to their employees. While HRD professionals are highly qualified presenters and facilitators, this is an inappropriate strategy as they are not held accountable for improving employee performance, nor are they responsible for conducting developmental evaluations designed or used to create performance growth and development plans. Furthermore, HRD professionals are not in a position to provide performance feedback and reinforcement so critical to learning transfer. The only members of the organization responsible for these essential activities are managers. Therefore, we strongly believe that organizations must shift

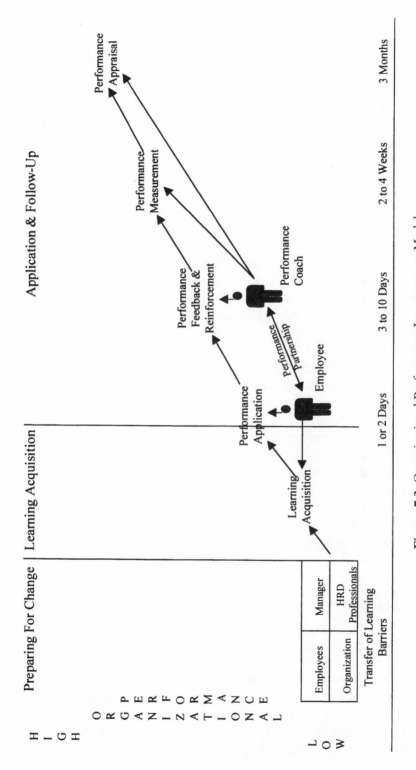

Figure 7.3 Organizational Performance Improvement Model

Gilley, J. W., & Maycunich, A., (1998), *Strategically Integrated HRD: Partnering to Maximize Organizational Performance*, Perseus Books.

the responsibility of training to managers and allow HRD professionals to serve their organizations as performance and organizational development consultants (see Chapter 5). Unfortunately, too many organizations still rely on the services of their HRD professionals as "trainers." Consequently, they sometimes produce barriers that prevent learning transfer, including failure to allow all members of the organization to participate in performance improvement activities, create results-driven training and development programs, or design training activities linked to the strategic business goals and objectives of the organization.

Fourth, employees must identify the completion date for each performance objective. Establishing a completion date provides employees with time-based parameters that are important when planning learning events. They also furnish a target date for learning acquisition and application, without which employees would postpone learning indefinitely.

Fifth, the final step of the learning acquisition and transfer plan is fairly easy and straightforward. It includes gathering performance improvement data that demonstrate growth and development, and comparing these data to performance standards and with an employee's performance baseline to determine the amount and degree of improvement. This analysis determines whether employees' performance objectives have been achieved.

The primary objective of a learning acquisition and transfer plan is to improve employee performance. Learning must be measured to ensure that employees achieve their performance objectives, change their performance behaviors, and enhance organizational effectiveness. It is extremely important that all organizational development activities be measured against the previously discussed criteria. In this way, concrete evidence exists that performance improvement occurs and business results improve.

CONCLUSION

Performance growth and development does not "simply happen"—it must be acquired through the concerted efforts of both managers and employees. Managers are charged with carefully considering the types of activities that improve employees' commitment and motivation. They must forge a partnership with employees designed to improve their performance and identify ways to enhance their employees' self-esteem, which will ultimately improve the organization and its results.

Managers must master the process of delegating work tasks and responsibilities to employees, while allowing employees to build on strengths while managing weaknesses. Finally, managers and employees, together, must design, develop, implement, and evaluate learning acquisition and transfer in such a way so as to produce desired performance growth and development outcomes.

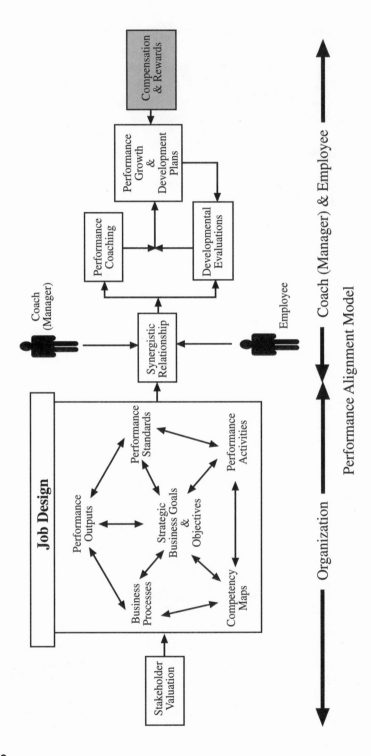

Performance Alignment Model

Chapter 8

LINKING COMPENSATION AND REWARDS TO PERFORMANCE GROWTH AND DEVELOPMENT

The purpose of any organization is to secure results, from increasing market share or sales revenue to improving quality or profitability. The responsibility for securing desired results lay with members of the management team, whose sole challenge is to "get results through people." Therefore, it makes tremendous sense to reward people for their growth, development, and commitment. This simple philosophy works wonders in improving employee performance and achieving the results needed by the organization.

Historically, compensation and reward programs have been performance-based, with little consideration given to rewarding employees for enhancing their skills and competencies. Nevertheless, employee performance increases dramatically if an organization links the compensation and reward program to employee performance growth and development activities. In this way, compensation and rewards become a vehicle for ever-increasing employee development as opposed to mere performance achievement. The intent is not to mitigate the importance of performance, but to make it clear that performance without growth and development will stagnate or even decline. Shifting compensation and reward programs to encourage employee growth and development ensures that employees' skills and competencies continue to evolve.

Improving organizational performance, productivity, and effectiveness remains a difficult undertaking, requiring the cooperation of the organization, its managers, and its employees. One of the best ways of improving organizational performance capacity is by linking compensation and rewards to the growth and development of employees. When these results are rewarded and reinforced they will be repeated. In this way, organizations encourage employees to develop their performance competencies such that they will be better able to produce desired results. Another outgrowth is that it enhances employees' commitment and loyalty. This straightforward, commonsense approach improves employee performance, involvement, and development. By becoming development-oriented, organizations adopt an approach that will help them systematically respond to the performance challenge.

DEVELOPING A COMPENSATION AND REWARDS PHILOSOPHY

Of critical importance to any organization is the formulation of a compensation and reward philosophy that anchors development of long-term compensation and reward strategies. This philosophy should link compensation and rewards to employee growth and development, thus enhancing organizational performance capacity.

Establishing a compensation and reward philosophy should be based on rewarding people for the "right" performance. In other words, organizations must understand that "the things that get rewarded get done" (LeBoeuf, 1985, p. 9). This assures that the organization will secure the desired results. Likewise, failure to reward the right behaviors leads to unsatisfactory results.

Another important component of a compensation and reward philosophy is its ability to take into account the organization's culture, values, guiding principles, and strategic business goals and objectives. Without this alignment, compensation and reward systems are doomed to fail.

A compensation and reward philosophy should be flexible enough to take into account the ever-changing nature of the organization, allowing linkage among compensation and rewards, change initiatives, and other important organization-wide activities. When this occurs, the compensation and reward program remains flexible, subject to review, alteration, or redesign—an approach that guarantees continuous compensation improvement.

An effective compensation and reward philosophy defines who participates in compensation and reward decisions, whether decision making should be centralized in the HR department or decentralized within departments, divisions, or units, and whether executives, managers, and supervisors should be held accountable for their respective decisions and contributions to the compensation and reward program (Flannery, Hofrichter, & Platten, 1996). The approach selected should be based on the philosophy that is most appropriate to the organization.

The compensation and reward philosophy should take into account each step of the performance alignment process. In this way, a compensation and reward approach is developed that allows organizations to identify stakeholder needs and expectations, design jobs that produce maximum results at the highest possible level of quality, encourage managers to build synergistic relationships with employees and make the transformation to performance coaches, require managers to conduct formal developmental evaluations with employees, and collaboratively create performance growth and development plans designed to enhance performance capacity.

LINKING COMPENSATION AND REWARDS TO GUIDING PRINCIPLES

Every organization adheres to a set of guiding principles. These principles serve as anchors during turbulent times and as rudders to negotiate difficult organizational seas. They also help organizations make strategic decisions, allocate resources, embrace change initiatives, and focus their efforts. Guiding principles should be based on the collective values of every member of the organization. Moreover, guiding principles offer an invisible hand, organizing and shepherding scattered employees in a singular direction to help the organization achieve its strategic mission. They serve as beacons on moonless nights when it appears the organization's future is darkest.

Because guiding principles are so essential to the direction and future of every organization, compensation and reward programs should be linked to them. While guiding principles may not indicate the organization's structure, they provide insight into how decisions are made within the firm and how the organization is managed. They also help identify the organization's strategic intent and how resources are allocated to achieve desired business results. Guiding principles identify how people are perceived within the organization and how senior management values their commitment, involvement, and contributions. Finally, they indicate whether the organization is dedicated to the growth and development of its people and rewarding them accordingly.

When linking compensation and rewards to the organization's guiding principles, the program must be designed to work in harmony with other vital systems within the firm. This linkage ensures the consistent allocation of compensation and rewards, helping the organization function in a way that is acceptable to senior executives and managers. Avoided are the numerous, inconsistent changes that occur when organizations attempt to blindly incorporate insufficient motivation strategies and employee retention techniques. Finally, this linkage guarantees that the compensation and reward system selected helps the organization achieve its desires.

SELECTING COMPENSATION AND REWARD STRATEGIES

Compensation and reward programs should be designed to help organizations achieve specific outcomes. Therefore, it is extremely important that organizations identify the compensation and reward strategies that will be most effective in achieving their desired results. They should also be selected specifically to address why organizations and employees fail to achieve desired performance results. As discussed in Chapter 1, employees fail to achieve desired results because:

- they are not rewarded for doing their jobs (reason 16)
- they are rewarded for doing less important activities (reason 17)
- they are asked to do one thing (i.e., work as a team) but are rewarded for another (i.e., individual compensation and bonuses) (reason 18, see Figure 1.3).

Organizations, on the other hand, fail to achieve necessary results because they do not focus on long-term achievements (reason 7, see Figure 1.2). The performance alignment process provides an excellent means of addressing these failures.

To ensure satisfactory results, appropriate compensation and reward strategies focus on: (1) long-term solutions, (2) entrepreneurship, (3) leadership, (4) employee performance growth and development, (5) teamwork and cooperation, (6) creativity, and (7) employee commitment and loyalty.

Strategy 1: Rewarding Long-term Solutions

Many organizations focus solely on quarterly or monthly results, compensating and rewarding employees accordingly. Moreover, organizational leaders are under extreme pressure to produce short-term results that satisfy stockholders, directors, and senior executives. This emphasis harms the organization's effectiveness, as it requires managers and employees to make decisions that encourage short-term gain at the expense of long-term strategic organizational health. To overcome this short-term phenomenon, organizations must adopt compensation and reward strategies to meet long-term goals. Then and only then will they focus on meaningful and sustainable business outcomes that will nourish the organization for many years to come.

To accomplish this, organizations must be willing to let managers and employees make decisions that encourage long-term organizational development and change, while discouraging those projects and activities that feed ravenous appetites for profitability. This change will dramatically affect the types of decisions made by managers and employees while fostering commonsense decision making and forward thinking.

Strategy 2: Rewarding Entrepreneurship

Employees should be encouraged to discover ways to improve business processes and performance activities. They should be rewarded for risk taking and decisive actions that improve organizational efficiency and effectiveness. Employees should be encouraged to act on their convictions and beliefs, and be supported by their managers when such decisions are made. When these behaviors are rewarded, employees will actively, even aggressively, produce more positive results.

Success and failure often depend on the degree of freedom employees enjoy. Employees who operate as entrepreneurs can and do energize others, creating an atmosphere of positive dynamism. Consequently, organizations should establish compensation and reward programs that reward entrepreneurial behavior.

Another aspect of rewarding entrepreneurship involves encouraging employees to apply new skills and knowledge on the job, in spite of the potential risk of their failure to produce the outcomes desired. According to Gilley and Boughton (1996), failure is one of the best learning experiences an employee can have. While allowing employees to experiment on the job, managers are helping them develop an ownership attitude that enhances employee commitment and involvement. When organizations reward entrepreneurship, they encourage employees to take intelligent risks that may lead to better business results.

Strategy 3: Rewarding Leadership

Too many managers and employees are comfortable as followers rather than leaders—content to let others make decisions about the direction of the organization or implement actions that steer the organization accordingly. This mind-set prevents talented, qualified employees and managers from making contributions that improve the overall effectiveness of the organization. While many firms encourage leadership, they seldom reward it. As a result, leadership vacuums exist in many of today's organizations. To overcome this dilemma, organizations must compensate and reward individuals who take risks, offer opinions, and make suggestions to better the organization. Some managers discourage this practice due to the fear that others will supersede their power and authority within the organization. They operate as though others' opinions and ideas are less important and less valuable than their own. Organizations must guard against appointing these individuals to leadership roles as they only serve to diminish employee involvement and commitment. In addition, organizations encourage managerial malpractice when these individuals have the opportunity to gatekeep opinions and ideas.

Strategy 4: Rewarding Employee Performance Growth and Development

Developmental organizations understand that investing in their people results in a bountiful harvest of business results. These organizations understand that without their people they could not achieve the results they do, provide quality service to their customers, or exercise strong leadership in the marketplace. Employees are the organization's greatest asset; therefore, organizations must develop long-term compensation and reward strategies that encourage them to participate in performance growth and development activities that foster continuous learning and skill acquisition. This strategy should reward employees for applying what they have learned on the job *and* reward managers and supervisors who create environments conducive to learning transfer. By rewarding performance growth and development, organizations nurture environments of continuous improvement, quality enhancement, and performance simplification; furthermore, production efficiencies become an operational reality rather than mere slogans or diatribes. Encouraging growth and development indicates an organization's readiness to reinforce and encourage employees who show the initiative to become all that they can.

Strategy 5: Rewarding Teamwork and Cooperation

Many organizations talk the talk but cannot walk the walk. On the surface, organizational rhetoric encourages teamwork and cooperation, advocating its importance and value in helping the organization achieve better business results. However, employees are confused as their companies continue to compensate and reward individual efforts and contributions. If organizations desire teamwork and cooperation they need to create reward strategies designed to bring about better team efforts and contributions. If organizations are serious about enhancing teamwork and cooperation, they must reward people for helping each other rather than continuing to foster a competitive, counterproductive environment that reduces employees' self-esteem. Teams win together and lose together, play together and struggle together—therefore, they should be rewarded together. Then and only then will employees be willing to give up the attitude of "what's in it for me" and adopt a "we attitude" characteristic of cooperation and esprit de corps.

Strategy 6: Rewarding Creativity

Organizations sometimes wonder why seasoned, tenured employees fail to share their ideas and opinions. Why are employees comfortable with the status quo, content to merely perform on the job day after day? These organizations often blame employees for their lack of participation and information sharing, discounting their intellectual creative abilities. They seldom look inward to discover whether they have established policies and procedures that prevent the sharing of creative ideas. Some organizations, such as Microsoft and 3M Corporation, understand the importance of encouraging and rewarding employees who share their innovations. Their Eleventh Commandment, *Thou Shalt Not Kill a New Product Idea*, serves as an inducement to employees to share their creative insights.

Unfortunately, some organizations gatekeep new, creative, innovative ideas that are quickly rejected as not feasible or practical. When a new idea *is* accepted, the employee rarely gets rewarded proportionately for the idea's worth. To overcome the creativity desert, organizations must develop climates that encourage new ideas and make innovation part of every employee's job. Several major principles are necessary to establish an innovative climate. According to LeBoeuf (1985), they include the following:

1. tolerate failure
2. create a relaxed, informal work environment
3. pay royalties for successful innovations and ideas
4. encourage friendly, supportive competition
5. support fantasy and unorthodox ideas

6. solicit employee involvement and participation
7. teach employees the basics of creative thinking and idea generation

Strategy 7: Rewarding Employee Commitment and Loyalty

Many organizations are guilty of the unpardonable sin of hiring new employees to perform identical jobs and paying them significantly more than current employees. All three authors have experienced this phenomenon during their careers, and remember how very angry, disenfranchised, demoralized, discouraged, and violated we felt when a colleague was hired to do the same job for more money. In each of our cases, the organizations violated our trust by providing insignificant rationales for their decisions. We were never able to secure satisfactory answers as to why our companies elected to behave in this manner. In each case, we left our respective organizations within two years of the incidents.

Organizations expect, even demand, loyalty and commitment, but rarely examine their own policies and procedures or compensation and reward programs to determine whether they are practicing hypocrisy. It is not enough to *expect* loyalty and commitment; organizations must also *give* it. An exemplary organization is Delta Airlines, whose philosophy statement supports loyalty and commitment:

> To belong to an organization that cares about them, challenges them, believes in them, and wants the best for them, not just as employees but as total human beings. (LeBoeuf, 1985, p. 59)

This statement recognizes the importance of individuals, not just as employees but as human beings. Most employees are willing to endure financial hardship if their organizations reciprocate with trustworthy intentions.

An organization's compensation and reward strategy communicates its underlying intentions for employees. When an organization is willing to invest in and reward employee performance growth and development, it is, in essence, communicating its employees' importance to the execution of the business plan.

Business success is a journey that all organizational members take together. Organizations provide job security, appropriate work environments, promotion and growth opportunities, and a fair, livable wage. In return, employees should be loyal and committed to the betterment of the organization as a whole. One important principle must be understood in order for organizations to adopt appropriate reward strategies: respect begets respect, loyalty begets loyalty, commitment begets commitments, and involvement begets involvement. It's that simple.

IDENTIFYING PERFORMANCE GROWTH AND DEVELOPMENT GOALS

Once an organization has identified its most appropriate performance reward strategies, managers working collaboratively with their employees should identify performance growth and development goals. Each goal must help an employee achieve one or more of the organization's strategic business goals and objectives. In this way, there is a direct link between the learning acquisition and transfer plans and the realization of business results. That is, learning acquisition and transfer plans are linked to an organization's strategic goals and objectives. In this way, performance growth and development becomes a performance enhancement activity that improves the organization's efficiency and effectiveness.

Employees' performance growth and development goals must be specific, measurable, agreed-on, realistic, and timely (SMART). These same criteria can be used when writing performance growth and development goals. These criteria guide construction of well-written strategic goals.

IDENTIFYING REWARDS THAT ENHANCE EMPLOYEE GROWTH AND DEVELOPMENT

Several rewards are particularly useful in motivating employees to participate in growth and development activities designed to improve their overall performance. Following are some of the most effective:

- financial compensation—money attached to achieving improved business performance as a result of increased knowledge or skills
- recognition for successfully completing performance growth and development plans
- gifts or prizes for achieving desired developmental outcomes
- sabbaticals for increased effort toward growth and development
- challenging or high-profile projects intended to advance employees or promote them within the organization

- promotions or job advancements linked to performance growth and development
- advanced titles or position status in lieu of financial compensation for improved performance growth and development

INTEGRATING COMPONENTS OF AN EFFECTIVE COMPENSATION AND REWARD PROGRAM

Seven components comprise an effective compensation program (Figure 8.1), each of which is directly or indirectly linked to the organization's reward strategy. In this way, each component is connected to a long-term strategic approach to improving organizational effectiveness. The components include goal setting, learning, expectations, growth and development, reinforcement and feedback, performance improvement, and performance standards.

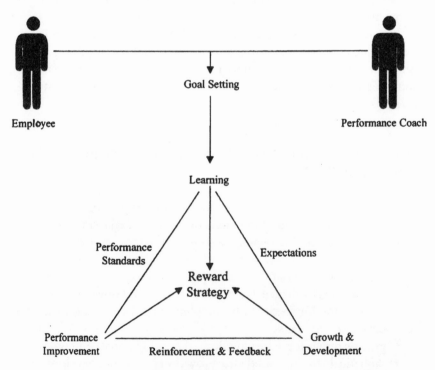

Figure 8.1 Components of an Effective Compensation and Reward Program

Effective compensation programs are initiated by setting perform-ance goals that employees are responsible for achieving—a collabora-tive activity between employees and their performance coaches. At its conclusion, employees should have developed several specific, measur-able, attainable, realistic, and time-based performance goals.

Once performance goals are identified, employees should engage in the process of identifying the learning that must occur in order for them to achieve their performance goals (see Chapter 7). By learning, we mean the specific knowledge and skills that must be acquired to accom-plish their goals. To complete this activity, employees should interact with their performance coach and peers to solicit their advice and rec-ommendations on "what it will take" to reach their goals.

To transform learning from an academic exercise into a real effort that produces growth and development, performance coaches must share their performance expectations with employees. That is, performance coaches must communicate what they expect their employees to be able to do differently as a result of learning and what specific outcomes are anticipated. These expectations may be in the form of measurable per-formance outputs, improved execution of performance activities, or demonstrations of new knowledge or skills. By establishing and com-municating expectations, employee learning becomes more focused, meaningful, and valuable.

Performance coaches provide employees with the standards by which performance outputs and activities will be measured and evaluated. These standards serve as targets for employees as they attempt to acquire and integrate new learning. Once learning has been converted into new be-haviors, employees should be able to demonstrate improved perform-ance in terms of outputs or activities.

Performance improvement and growth and development are two anchors of effective compensation and reward programs (Figure 8.1). Without them, there would be no real, tangible outcomes by which to attach increased compensation and rewards. That is, performance goals that are linked to an organization's reward strategy must produce some type of measurable outcomes that help the organization achieve its strategic business goals and objectives. Moreover, employee efforts to acquire new learning must result in performance improvement on the job or growth and development that increase overall organizational per-formance capacity. In either case, learning must be transferred to the job and demonstrated as performance improvement, or expended to the organization via the aggregate of employee growth and development.

Regardless, the organization benefits from employee learning acquisition; therefore, employees should be compensated and rewarded.

A common denominator of both performance improvement and employee growth and development is reinforcement and feedback. Without this component, performance improvement and employee growth and development are not likely to occur. Since the importance of this activity has been previously discussed (Chapters 5 and 6), we will only provide emphasis here.

While each of the seven components is important in the application of a compensation and reward program, emphasis on individual components varies depending on the purpose of learning. For example, if an employee establishes a performance goal designed to improve performance on the job during the next six months, it would be most appropriate to proceed from the top down, counterclockwise, focusing on learning acquisition and the role performance standards play in performance improvement (Figure 8.1). In this way, employees are practicing new skills or using new knowledge to improve the delivery of performance outputs or the execution of performance activities—both of which are linked to performance standards (Figure 8.1). Therefore, performance standards measure the depth and breadth of learning and its application to the job.

As performance improves, coaches should provide positive reinforcement and feedback that, over time, will deepen learning acquisition while helping employees achieve overall growth and development.

When an employee establishes a performance goal designed to enhance his or her growth and development, the outcome is long term-oriented. Thus, it is important to proceed from the top down, clockwise, identifying the performance coach's expectations of how learning is to be used and how it fits into an employee's career development (Figure 8.1). While learning of this type is not intended to improve an employee's immediate performance, it may have a profoundly positive impact on productivity if reinforced. As a result, long-term growth and development plans often yield positive short-term effects.

An effective compensation and reward program incorporates seven integrated components, each of which compels employees to acquire learning. Each component is linked to an overall compensation and reward strategy that helps it achieve desired business results. In the final analysis, learning acquisition and transfer must be rewarded to ensure continuation. In this way, compensation and reward programs are meaningful and valuable, and continually produce positive organizational results.

LINKING COMPENSATION AND REWARDS TO PERFORMANCE GROWTH AND DEVELOPMENT OUTCOMES

Figure 8.2 outlines the steps managers follow when linking compensation and rewards to performance growth and development outcomes. First, organizations select a reward strategy(s) they wish to employ via their compensation and reward program. This step provides an organization with a strategic focus for the compensation and reward process. In this way, organizations identify the long-term organizational results they wish to achieve.

Second, managers compare employees' performance growth and development goals with identified reward strategies to determine their congruence. In other words, employees' performance growth and development goals must match the organization's reward strategy or the organization will reward activities that are not designed to achieve its long-term goals and objectives. If these two components are incompatible, adjustments must be made in the organization's reward strategy, employees' performance growth and development goals, or both. This step ensures that the organization's long-term reward strategy is compatible with employee development activities.

Third, managers must make certain that employee' performance growth and development goals are specific, measurable, agreed-on, realistic, and timely (SMART). If for some reason these goals fail to meet such criteria, they should be reevaluated, reclarified, and rewritten.

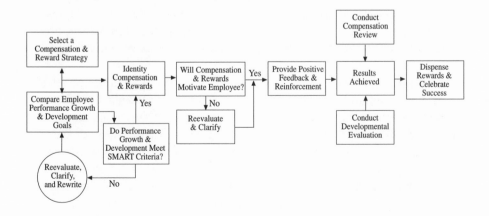

Figure 8.2 Applying Compensation and Rewards

Fourth, rewards that motivate employees to participate in performance growth and development activities require identification. These rewards may include financial compensation (money), merit pay, profit sharing, gainsharing, bonuses, or group incentives. Nonmonetary rewards include recognition, sabbaticals, promotions or advancement, freedom and independence, or prizes. Rewards must be substantial enough to motivate employees to continue professional development activities.

Fifth, managers must ascertain whether identified rewards indeed motivate employees. This can be accomplished through a variety of evaluation techniques, including focus groups, personal interviews, questionnaires, or small group discussions. If rewards fail to motivate employee participation in professional development activities, they should be reevaluated or clarified.

Sixth, employees need positive feedback and reinforcement to guarantee their motivation to acquire new skills and competencies and transfer them to the job. Regardless of the organization's compensation and reward strategy or employees' goals, the appropriateness of rewards, positive feedback and reinforcement powerfully encourage employee participation and involvement.

Seventh, once results have been achieved, managers conduct developmental evaluations and compensation reviews. As discussed in Chapter 6, developmental evaluations analyze, assess, and measure employee performance against performance standards. They also identify performance growth and development opportunities. Performance reviews are formal discussions between managers and employees that identify the type of compensation and rewards that will be granted for exemplary performance. This review activity is less developmental in nature, primarily focused on determining the amount and type of rewards to be disbursed.

Eighth, once developmental evaluations and compensation reviews have been conducted, managers dispense employee rewards accordingly and celebrate their successes. At the conclusion of this step, managers should evaluate the entire process to determine whether the organization's reward strategies have been achieved. Furthermore, they should examine whether employees' performance growth and development goals have been rewarded appropriately and whether the performance enhancements desired have been achieved.

The purpose of this framework is to provide managers with a step-by-step guide that links the compensation and reward program to employee performance growth and development goals. The guide incorporates many of the same components that comprise the performance management process, such as providing positive feedback and reinforcement, conducting developmental evaluations, and conducting compensation reviews. This guide is not designed to replace the performance management process but to help managers discover ways of rewarding employee growth and development. This guide also makes certain that organizations have a clearly identified and defensible reward strategy for achieving desired business results.

CONCLUSION

Developmental organizations believe that their success is directly related to their employees' growth and development. They compensate and reward employees for performance achievements as well as growth and development. Simultaneously, performance improvement and employee development become equal partners in the organization's success equation. Developmental organizations embrace the use of performance alignment processes that enable employees to become the organization's greatest asset. They encourage managers to make the transition to performance coaches, allowing them to serve as trainers, confronters, mentors, and counselors. Managers provide positive feedback and reinforcement to improve skills and competencies that ultimately improve employees' overall performance.

Developmental organizations assist managers in transforming traditional performance appraisal activities into developmental evaluations used to analyze, assess, and measure performance as well as to identify professional development needs. Developmental organizations encourage managers and employees to collaboratively design growth and development plans for performance enhancement. Finally, they link compensation and reward programs to performance growth and development outcomes.

Chapter 9

DEVELOPING LEADERSHIP EFFECTIVENESS

The performance alignment model is an excellent tool for addressing the performance challenge. Two additional strategies are also useful when transforming employees into the organization's greatest asset. First, organizations must improve their leadership quality by selecting and training leaders who can either demonstrate or develop the skills and competencies needed to build positive working relationships with employees that maximize business results. Second, organizations must make the evolution from traditional work groups responsible for providing everyday performance outputs to virtual teams accountable for collaborative, creative problem solving (see Chapter 10).

Improving leadership quality and utilizing virtual teams enables organizations to enforce strategies that foster meaningful change that positively positions employees within the organization. Moreover, these strategies bring about results that improve organizational performance capacity. Consequently, employees will be viewed as vital assets, essential to enhancing organizational competitiveness and profitability.

LEADERSHIP EFFECTIVENESS MODEL

When examining leadership's impact on an organization's ability to address the performance challenge, four critical competencies surface, demonstrating behaviors that help organizations transcend the gulf of performance despair. These competencies help leaders transform traditional, short term-oriented organizations into developmental organizations (see Chapter 11). The four competencies that provide the foundation for improving leadership quality are **critical reflective skills, strategic thinking skills, interpersonal skills, and performance-enhancing skills** (Figure 9.1). Within each of the four competencies, several supporting competencies provide a foundation for leadership effectiveness.

	Relationship-Driven	Organizationally Driven
Conceptual	Critical Reflective Skills	Strategic Thinking Skills
Practical	Interpersonal Skills	Performance-Enhancing Skills

Figure 9.1 Leadership Effectiveness Model

These competencies collectively comprise the leadership effectiveness model that is based on four separate but interrelated concepts and ideas. First, effective leaders function on two separate levels, the conceptual (macro) level and the practical (employee) level. The conceptual level refers to the strategic, long term-oriented, visionary plane on which leaders operate. The practical level refers to the daily activities for which leaders are responsible within their organizations. Second, leaders must be simultaneously relationship-oriented and organizationally performance-oriented. Relationship orientation refers to the ability of a leader to interact with employees, managers, and other executives. Organizational performance orientation refers to the achievement of business results that enable the organization to maintain financial viability.

Critical Reflective Skills

Effective leaders possess the innate ability to examine their behaviors and beliefs and make appropriate adjustments. In essence, they reinvent themselves over and over again. To be successful, they must possess critical reflective skills—the ability to look inward to discover new awarenesses and insights. Consequently, these leaders are extremely effective in building and maintaining working relationships—a skill that is philosophical and abstract in nature.

For organizations to maintain a consistent focus and direction, leaders must possess the capacity to understand who they are and what they believe, and be able to identify their strengths and weaknesses. Most successful leaders throughout history (including business) are those individuals who are self-aware. We define critical reflectiveness as the ability to understand one's values and beliefs, and to know why one behaves in a particular manner. Leaders sometimes are required to adapt to situations and circumstances.

Critical reflectiveness implies that people understand "why" they alter their behavior and when these changes violate their basic values and beliefs. Critically reflective leaders, therefore, know when changes are consistent with their guiding principles and when they are not. Without this self-awareness competency, leaders have difficulty motivating employees, as they are perceived as lacking personal integrity. Two competencies support critical reflectiveness: value alignment and adaptability.

Value alignment Value alignment is the integration of an individual's guiding principles (values and beliefs) with those of the organization. The first step in creating this alignment is for leaders to understand what personal principles they hold important and to compare them with those of the organization. The following questions will help:

- What are your values?
- What are your organization's values?
- Do your values and beliefs link with the organization's values and beliefs?
- How do your values and beliefs impact daily interactions with employees?

When identifying values and beliefs, it is important to examine the things that have meaning in one's life, including family, friendships, exercise, nutrition, lifestyle, geographic location, and so on. Including these things in value alignment analysis better isolates those factors that drive behavior.

Examination of values allows leaders to enjoy their jobs and feel challenged. Making a list of values helps identify those things that hold importance for leaders at all organizational levels. These items must be considered when developing a value alignment analysis activity, as they drive the decision-making activities that direct the organization. Once the critical values that drive leaders' thought processes have been established, they must be aligned with the organization's values. Value alignment allows leaders to define a link between their values and those of the organization, laying the foundation for improving leadership effectiveness.

Adaptability While effective leaders adhere to a set of guiding principles that direct their behaviors and actions, they must also have an innate ability to adapt their behavior to any given situation. Adapting to circumstances, events, or situations is critical to effective leadership.

Change is one factor that exists in every organization. Organizational leaders who effectively meet the demands of change are better suited for creating performance environments where employees flourish. By embracing change and preparing for it, leaders are able to make appropriate adjustments in their behavior, which helps meet the needs of their employees. Being able to adapt to change is of paramount importance for effective leadership.

In Chapter 4, we discussed the importance of acceptance and building synergistic relationships. To become an effective leader, one must be able to accept the divergent views and behaviors existing within the organization. Recently, we worked with a senior manager who had been promoted to oversee the organization's technical division. She had an extremely difficult time interacting with highly technical employees. These individuals could analyze complicated diagrams and perform complex research calculations and analysis, but could not communicate this information in a practical, easily understood manner. The senior manager became very frustrated with this behavior and often showed it when interacting with these employees. As a result, she was losing their respect and support, and diminishing her credibility within the organization.

We were able to identify a variety of ways for her to adapt her style in order to successfully interact with these technical wizards, such as:

- researching material ahead of time
- learning their language
- comparing questions before interacting with technical employees
- role-playing the interaction with confidential employees in order to smooth out difficulties
- developing relationships with technical professionals off the job

When these tactics were employed, she was able to adapt her interaction with technical employees. She was able to enhance her credibility by using her expertise to build consensus within the team, which was a huge step in becoming a more effective leader. By adapting her behavior to the needs of her technical employees, she was able to regain her credibility and their respect.

This example demonstrates the positive impact of being adaptive. Some leaders, however, believe that it is the responsibility of their employees to adapt *their* behavior. Perhaps a reciprocal approach, where everyone attempts to adapt his or her behavior when appropriate, is most effective. Regardless, adaptability provides an opportunity to improve employee interaction and relationships. As a result, employees feel more comfortable discussing important issues that impact overall organizational effectiveness and ultimately help produce desired business outcomes. Finally, adaptability is a practical way to demonstrate self-awareness.

As we examine the remaining core competencies, self-reflectiveness surfaces as the foundation for effective leadership. Self-reflectiveness allows demonstration of understanding of the emotional needs of employees, which creates emotional alignment producing improved business results (see Chapter 1). Self-awareness, value alignment, and adaptability allow for demonstration of self-reflective skills, which are critical in understanding effective leadership and positively addressing the performance challenge.

Strategic Thinking Skills

Critical reflective skills provide the ability to look inward in order to understand emotions and feelings, while strategic thinking is the ability to look outside oneself and focus on the organization's future. Strategic thinking skills promote a work environment and culture that enable employees to achieve business success.

When leaders focus on the conceptual level to improve organizational performance, they must think strategically to positively impact business results. Strategic thinking includes the ability to anticipate business trends and processes, and break them down into manageable units for others to understand and implement. By successfully breaking down strategies into manageable components, effective leaders generate a variety of solutions that decrease the gap between what is needed and what is delivered. Effective leaders create a new paradigm for their organizations, communicating and coordinating activities that assess their respective products and services, and making the necessary adjustments internally. They also participate in the identification and visualization of strategies implemented throughout the organization.

Taking an inclusive approach with respect to strategic orientation avoids the pitfall of not getting buy-in from all employees and stakeholders. An inclusive, collaborative approach to strategy identification allows effective leaders to break down information, prioritize it, and recommend a step-by-step approach for implementation. Along the way, effective leaders adapt and make necessary changes for the successful completion of their strategies.

Strategic thinking is a critical component in successfully creating a vision that adds purpose to employees' organizational lives. A strategic approach enables employees to expedite the process that will provide the greatest business environment for success. An environment of continuous success provides positive experiences for employees, managers, and executives within the organization.

When a leader uses strategic thinking skills, he or she establishes a direction for the organization toward achieving the results needed to improve profitability, productivity, and effectiveness. Strategic thinking is a conceptual-level activity requiring leaders to establish organizational priorities (Figure 9.1). In this way, effective leaders create an organizational vision while accounting for the perceptions of others. Additionally, they must remain objective in order to identify practical ways of achieving their organization's purpose. Effective leaders possess the ability to look to the future and navigate uncharted waters. In short, effective leaders hold a clear vision of the future and use their objectivity to remain practically focused while understanding the impact of employees' perceptions on decision making. These represent the three critical supportive competencies of strategic thinking: organizational vision, objectivity, and perception.

Organizational vision Effective leaders have a clear vision for their organization, in terms of both its financial condition and human resources. Organizational vision helps focus scattered employees toward achieving a common set of outcomes that will determine their success or failure. The first step in creating a vision is to identify the purpose of the organization. Successful organizations clearly know what they want to achieve and how they want to serve their customers. Effective leaders are successful in communicating this purpose and developing a vision that ensures employee support and involvement.

In contrast, ineffective leaders have difficulty achieving buy-in from employees due to failure to adequately communicate their vision of the organization. Ineffective leaders often identify the organization's purpose but are unable to articulate its vision. In these organizations, vision statements are "just a bunch of words that have no meaning for those of us in the trenches." This sad commentary is due in part to lack of effective leadership. Poor leaders take more pride in creating well-written vision statements than in building acceptance among their employees for its execution.

To create a successful organizational vision, effective leaders must secure buy-in from all employees at the beginning of the process rather than after it has been written. Employees who have shared their opinions and ideas take ownership for their initiation and continuance.

Recently, we worked with an organization that allowed its employees to develop and implement a new organizational vision. We established focus groups that helped them identify the following:

- the organizational "big picture"
- organizational purpose
- stakeholders
- processes that needed to be changed
- strategies to be used in implementing the organizational vision

Employees were able to create a vision that they were willing to embrace. This approach is an extremely powerful process that dramatically impacts organizational productivity and profitability. Vision statements give employees' daily activities serious meaning.

Effective leaders utilize an inclusive approach to designing and developing organizational vision. Allowing employees to participate in the development of organizational vision enables them to accept the responsibility for making it happen. Effective leaders pragmatically communicate and receive the support necessary for the vision to resonate throughout the organization, thereby creating an environment of employee and organizational success.

Objectivity Guiding principles before personal agendas is the mantra of effective leaders. When looking at strategic thinking competencies, effective leaders need to keep in mind that their responsibility is to meet the needs and expectations of all organizational stakeholders. This is why it is critical for effective leaders not to focus on individual personalities, but instead on the guiding principles on which the organization is based. To achieve this end, effective leaders must remain objective, avoiding the political quicksand that exists in all organizations. We are not suggesting that these leaders hold an idealistic approach to business. Rather, we mean that they should remain objective and focused regarding their responsibilities to their stakeholders.

All too often, leaders lose their objectivity by taking sides based on their personal relationships with members of the organization. Keeping the organization's best interests in mind and remaining objective proves difficult, as some personalities are stronger and more forceful than others—often tending to be overbearing. Some organizational members dominate, pushing their positions onto others without regard to organizational impact. Leaders who are unable to remain objective can be steamrolled by strong personalities, and tend not to make informed decisions.

Objectivity remains elusive for some leaders who hold extremely passionate opinions. Effective leaders are those who are able to listen in a detached way, keeping their emotions out of interactions. They demonstrate patience by evaluating information and others' opinions carefully prior to rendering decisions. Effective leaders critique information carefully and step back to make certain that their responses are based on fact rather than emotion.

Perception All effective leaders must deal with the perceptions of those they interact with on a regular basis as well as those that they have never met. Some of these individuals may have favorable perceptions, others may not. Nevertheless, effective leaders refuse to allow others' perceptions to negatively affect them or create an environment full of paranoia or fear. They are able to rally employee support and keep employees focused on the purposes and goals of the organization.

Perceptions, whether positive or negative, are rarely founded on fact. Perceptions are based on limited experiences, beliefs, or chance encounters. For example, what is your perception of a life insurance or used car salesperson? If negative, does this mean that all of these salespersons are the same? Of course not. Random interactions are by no means representative of the entire sales population. On the other hand, what are your perceptions of a doctor or college professor? Most people hold doctors and college professors in great esteem, believing they are altruistic, with their patients' or students' best interests at heart. Is this a completely accurate view? Again, of course not. Sadly, some doctors' and college professors' motivations are not patient- or student-centered. Conversely, many salespersons are absolutely interested in their unique customers, displaying sincere commitment to satisfying their clients' wants or needs. These examples reveal how perceptions impact decision making.

Effective leaders do not permit their perceptions to negatively affect their decisions or solutions. They examine situations carefully and consider information without bias.

We have examined the two conceptual-level competencies of effective leadership. We've demonstrated the need for effective leaders to have a clear, holistic understanding of themselves and their organizations. Such insights enable leaders to improve business results and create developmental environments where their employees flourish. We will now examine the practical, hands-on levels of effective leadership—interpersonal skills and performance-enhancing skills.

Interpersonal Skills

Effective leaders possess strong interpersonal skills that allow them to motivate employees and achieve desired results. Interpersonal skills enhance leaders' abilities to deliver performance feedback (Chapter 5) and developmental evaluations (Chapter 6), conduct performance-confronting activities (Chapter 5), and provide counseling and mentoring (Chapter 5). Interpersonal skills are directed at the individual, and are used to engage personal conversations and discussions designed to improve employee relations (Figure 9.1). To demonstrate interpersonal skills, one must successfully perform four supportive competencies: team building, relationship building, communication skills, and empathy. These competencies enable leaders to successfully motivate and challenge their employees to continuously improve.

Team building In Chapter 10, we will discuss in great detail the role that teams play in the achievement of organizational success. Teams are a microcosm of the entire organization, demonstrating role relationships, job execution, performance feedback and evaluation, and reward strategies. Effective leaders identify and use teams in the execution of organizational vision and the achievement of critical business results. This is accomplished by allowing teams to explore problems and identify solutions to issues that prevent the organization from being successful. Effective teams are invaluable in reaching business goals and objectives. Leaders understand that creating a collaborative approach to problem solving commits employees to the organization's well-being and support of strategic initiatives (see Chapter 10).

To become team-oriented, leaders must understand that they don't have all the answers to questions that plague their organizations. Teams provide leaders with a deep reservoir of experience from which to draw in the formulation of solutions to organizational problems. Leaders neglect to use teams appropriately due to their fear of relinquishing decision-making control and unwillingness to explore alternative solutions. These ineffective leaders have failed to develop the critical reflective skills that promote lively debates regarding problem identification and resolution. Furthermore, ineffective leaders have not yet developed the type of trusting employee relationships needed to delegate control.

Relationship building Relationship building is absolutely key to everything discussed throughout this book. The performance challenge cannot be adequately addressed unless leaders develop positive relationships with employees—relationships that enhance employee commitment and involvement. The relationship model discussed in Chapter 4 is the foundation for nurturing continued growth and development of employees. Continuously working on synergistic relationships creates mutual respect with employees, an essential element of effective leadership.

By failing to develop positive working relationships, leaders limit their opportunities to generate the energy and momentum necessary for future business success. Working relationships are a fundamental component of day-to-day interaction with every employee. The next step involves examining techniques via which leaders effectively communicate with their peers, managers, and employees. By understanding communications, leaders gain valuable insight into ways of inspiring employees and allowing them to flourish even in extremely demanding environments.

Communications Effective leaders develop the ability to skillfully communicate with everyone throughout the organization. Unfortunately, communications is a bridge that many would-be leaders fail to cross. Communications is not just about how ideas are presented or the rhetorical choices made during a discourse, but is the ability to use all communications mechanisms available to stimulate and challenge employees to achieve greatness. Effective leaders are those who are able to communicate efficiently and consistently with employees, making certain that information is thoroughly distributed in a manner that is easily understood. Effective leaders display powerful nonverbal messages when interacting with their employees, allowing receivers to feel strong and decisive when decoding or formulating strategy.

The most critical tool utilized by effective leaders when communicating is listening. Listening can make or break an interaction. When individuals interact, leaders make three critical mistakes: (1) they develop responses before employees are finished, (2) they get distracted by other activities or events, and (3) they selectively listen to employees. These three mistakes cause distortions during interactions, allowing leaders to misinterpret information. Recall the telephone game, where information changes as the message passes from one individual to the next? As more people receive and transmit the information, it becomes more and more distorted. This can be the end result of any employee interaction unless leaders actively listen, engaging in techniques that ensure understanding. "Shut up and listen" seems particularly appropriate for executives, who often dominate interactions whether by choice or circumstance.

Another critical element of effective communications is the ability to ask pertinent questions. Questioning is one of the most impactful ways of showing that you are listening. By asking questions, you show an individual that you understand what he or she is saying. Effective questioning is a skill requiring commitment and practice. Fortunately, active listening encourages questioning as one's natural curiosity and desire for clarification surface.

One of the authors had the distinct pleasure and honor of working for Nora Ruder, vice president extraordinaire of Foremost Corporation of America, who exhibits some of the most powerful, effective communication skills we've witnessed. Nora meets with her "team" on a weekly basis, typically Monday mornings beginning at 8 A.M. The majority of time is spent listening to each member share, with the entire group, accomplishments of the past week and plans for the week ahead. A volunteer records responses on an easel pad, which allows comparisons of planned activities versus actual results. This process keeps all team members well apprised of each others' actions, strategies, and intentions. These weekly meetings also provide a regular forum for sharing information or concerns regarding individual, department, or corporate issues. As a result, team members are well informed, have equal opportunities to provide significant input, and feel more valued as employees.

In addition to weekly group meetings, Nora meets with each individual member of her team on a monthly basis. In these meetings, topics of discussion range from performance feedback to career paths to relevant personal issues. At one point or another Nora assumes all roles of the performance coach: trainer, confronter, mentor, and counselor. The result? The authors can personally attest to the benefits. An environment of respect, loyalty, commitment, and sense of worth permeates the department—which better prepares the team to meet the challenging demands of business.

For Nora, a combination of regular one-on-ones and group meetings ensures the adequate, timely flow of communication, which is one component of her employee-centered leadership style. She recognizes her employees' value, firmly championing their growth and development, both personal and professional. Effective communications is just the start.

Word killers Several "word killers" exist in communications; they are: *want, why,* and *but.* "Want" is used by individuals to gain control over others, creating a hierarchy and clearly indicating that the person using the word intends to dominate the interaction ("I want you to . . ."). We prefer use of the word "need" ("We need to . . .") which eliminates the hierarchy and creates a more even playing field between leaders and employees. "Need" builds self-esteem, reinforcing the individual's critical contribution to the work to be completed.

The use of "why" forces employees to defend their behavior or position. Asking "Why did you do that?" fixes blame and becomes very judgmental. Effective leaders tend to ask more "how" and "what" questions ("How will you . . . ?", "What can be done to . . . ?"), allowing employees to focus on ways of resolving the conflict or problem. Doing so encourages cooperation, which allows for positive interactions to occur. Using the words "why" or "want" is commensurate with cornering an angry pit bull, as most people have negative psychological reactions to these words.

The word with the greatest negative impact on organizations is "but." Ineffective leaders use this word to focus on the negative aspects of a conversation when they fear that something bad is about to happen ("That sounds all right, but . . ."). Employees shut down mentally when they hear this word and immediately go on the defensive. We suggest substituting the word "but" with "and"—or pausing and allowing employees to respond.

Communications is important for organizational success, and provides opportunities to demonstrate effective leadership skills. The keys to effective communications are to listen, ask questions, and be clear and concise. Each of these has been discussed in the last several pages—we challenge you to use effective communications skills when interacting with employees.

Occupying the executive suite does not make one an effective leader. One must make a commitment to self and the organization to communicate using interpersonal skills, build teams, and enhance relationships. Applying these competencies enables the creation of an environment where positive energy flows and open, honest discussions abound.

Empathy One of the critical tenets of interpersonal skills is empathy, which is the ability to understand the emotions, feelings, values, and beliefs of others. Effective leaders have the ability to read others' feelings and emotions, clearly understanding when people are upset, happy, sad, or confused. Combined with the innate ability to lead others, effective leaders generate outcomes that produce organizational results. In other words, reading people is of principal importance in promoting organizational success. By being able to understand the emotional needs of employees, effective leaders are able to direct them in areas that allow them to flourish.

Many ineffective leaders force their will and opinions onto others in order to produce short-term gains in productivity at the expense of demoralizing employees. This is a critical mistake that has a dramatically negative impact on organizational success. Lacking the ability to empathize, ineffective leaders stifle creativity, cooperation, and collaboration, any of which generally have very positive effects on the organization. These so-called leaders may generate favorable short-term financial results but over the long haul will negatively impact business results.

Performance-enhancing Skills

To be an effective leader, one must improve employee performance and productivity. As performance enhancers, leaders improve overall organization performance one employee at a time (Figure 9.1). That is, performance enhancers improve organizational results by improving the individual performance of each and every employee.

While it is important to increase the performance and productivity of employees, it must be done while maintaining their dignity and respect. Furthermore, performance improvement efforts must be linked to the organization's strategic business goals and objectives in order to positively impact the bottom line. When examining performance-enhancing skills, we will focus on the supporting competencies that allow business results to flourish. They are: understanding business operations, identifying one's work style, developing command skills that demonstrate respect, and achieving results. These competencies allow one to truly become an effective, diligent leader capable of maximizing each employee's performance.

Business acumen Improving organizational performance begins by having insight into the operational aspects of the business—that is, business acumen. By understanding how businesses operate, effective leaders promote initiatives that help the organization improve its competitiveness and profitability. They adapt developmental programs that motivate employees to increase their productivity and improve performance. Another way effective leaders demonstrate their business acumen is by understanding their stakeholders' needs and expectations. Once understood, effective leaders can adapt their processes, products, and services to better serve stakeholder interests.

Effective leaders must be long term-focused, resisting quick fix opportunities or short-term decisions that promise financial gain at the expense of organizational health. Effective leaders weather the financial storm by focusing on the big picture and by helping others see the benefit of long-term strategic solutions to complex problems.

Understanding stakeholders' needs and expectations, being aware of the financial and business issues facing the organization, and creating long-term solutions to difficult problems provide excellent opportunities to improve the organization's strength and viability. Having a keen awareness and a potent operational understanding of the business leverages one's knowledge and expertise to improve the organization's performance.

Work style An effective leader's work style allows him or her to successfully complete tasks and projects. Work style is the manner in which leaders meet the demands and responsibilities of the job. Three types of work styles predominate:

- directive
- supportive
- collaborative

Using directive work styles, leaders take charge of all job responsibilities, requesting minimal input from stakeholders. These leaders tend to be workaholics or perfectionists, driven to succeed. Sometimes, they surround themselves with people who have little experience or expertise so they can control workflow and decision making. Occasionally, these leaders overcompensate for their lack of interpersonal skills by exceeding their personal goals and objectives.

Supportive work style leaders encourage the creativity and entrepreneurial skills and abilities of their employees. They become employee advocates, giving them every opportunity to achieve success. Under this work style, employees often possess a great deal of experience and expertise, needing little direction to complete job-related tasks.

The collaborative work style is punctuated by leaders and employees working together to accomplish the organization's goals and objectives. Under these circumstances, true performance synergy can be achieved as the talents, skills, abilities, and expertise of each employee are utilized for the good of the organization. These work environments are very conducive to formulating sharing, creative, and energetic solutions to problems facing the organization. When a collaborative work style is used, work teams tend to have a high degree of stability, maturity, and knowledge of organizational strategy.

We have worked with a variety of leaders in a number of organizations, and have consistently found the most effective ones adapt their work style to meet the needs of their people and the organization. Effective leaders are acutely aware of their employees' maturity and skill levels, and appropriately adjust their work styles to ensure organizational success. Consequently, none of the work styles previously discussed are any better than any other. While they all have respective strengths and weaknesses, the one selected should be the most appropriate for the situation, project, and employees' needs.

Commanding with respect Effective leaders are well respected by their people. Leaders earn respect through hard work, fairness, honesty, and devotion to the organization's guiding principles. Leadership without respect is like taking advice for raising your children from someone who has never had kids. The individual giving advice has little or no credibility with regard to child rearing. As a result, his or her knowledge, insight, or opinions are not respected. Over time these opinions are discounted, eventually being ruled out altogether. Leaders are in similar situations when they fail to gain their employees' respect. Regardless of the leaders' knowledge and experience, unless they are respected, employees will dismiss their recommendations, suggestions, and advice.

All too often leaders use extremely divisive measures to control and manipulate their employees. We saw this occur in an organization we recently worked with. We were helping them test a 360-degree feedback tool that was to be distributed to all employees to gauge leadership effectiveness. One executive received some negative feedback and was so angry that he pulled his team together and berated them for their responses. He said, "The organization doesn't care what you said about me because they're happy with the results that I have delivered and if you don't like it then you can get the hell out of here." This organization and this executive need help. As you can imagine, morale throughout the organization was terrible, and they were spending millions of dollars recruiting, hiring, and selecting employees because they were losing over 60 percent of new hires within two years. They were lacking effective leadership and were allowing managerial malpractice to run rampant.

Command with respect is a difficult skill to master. Leading with respect is one of the most effective ways of motivating and inspiring employees. Effective leaders focus their ambition and passion on meeting their employees' emotional needs and demonstrating mutual respect for their contributions and efforts. The result will be improved organizational effectiveness, performance, and productivity.

Achieving results Achieving results is the final competency we will discuss and the pinnacle of leadership effectiveness. The bottom line is that organizational leaders possess the ultimate responsibility to secure results through people. Failing to achieve desired results means that leaders have failed to lead. Effective leaders are responsible for creating environments where their employees challenge the status quo, engage in creative, lively debates designed to identify efficiencies, produce creative solutions to difficult problems, and participate in continuous organizational improvement. In fact, creating such an environment is indicative of effective leadership.

USING EXECUTIVE COACHING TO DEVELOP LEADERSHIP EFFECTIVENESS SKILLS

One of the most effective means of developing effective leadership skills is to conduct executive coaching activities with senior managers. According to Witherspoon and White (1997), executive coaching can be used in four ways to develop senior managers and executives. First, executive coaching can enhance skills used in their current jobs. Second, executive coaching can improve performance in their present jobs. Third, it can be developmental, as in preparation for a future job. Fourth, executive coaching can focus on enhancing a senior manager's or executive's leadership agenda, which in the broadest sense encompasses furthering the ideas, opinions, and activities that executives perceive to be most important.

According to Catherine Lawrence, vice president of Executive Development for Fidelity Management and Research Company, executive coaching is most successful when it is used as a "just in time" learning activity, enabling executives to learn skills and develop competencies that are meaningful and valuable to them. She contends that executive coaching should be a private, individualized activity customized to the needs and expectations of each executive. She also maintains that executive coaching is short term-oriented and relationship-based. Finally, executive coaching is most effective when it is results-oriented.

The Fidelity Management and Research Company has identified a five-step process useful in determining if executive coaching is an appropriate activity. An organization should:

1. Describe its business needs and current situation.
2. Describe the individual's development needs and how they impact the organization.
3. Describe what the individual will do differently as a result of improvement and what will be the impact on the organization.
4. Determine if there is a similar pattern within the organization. If so, executive coaching is not appropriate; however, an organizational development intervention may be.
5. Determine whether key stakeholders believe there is a developmental need. If so, executive coaching is recommended. If not,

meet with stakeholders to determine appropriate steps (Lawrence, 1998).

Executive coaching is an excellent strategy for enhancing the leadership skills and competencies necessary to help organizations address the performance challenge. By doing so, organizations make the commitment to improving the current skills, performance capacity, and developmental opportunities of their executives in such a way that executives can appropriately perform their current jobs as well as future appointments within the organization.

CONCLUSION

Creating work environments where employees flourish and strive for excellence separates effective leaders from ineffective ones. Effective leaders understand who they are, adapting their skills to meet the needs of people within their organizations. They possess an abundance of energy that they channel to build the self-esteem of those around them. Effective leaders create an organizational vision and strategy for achieving it, utilizing their employees' knowledge and skills while encouraging stimulating discourse that challenges the status quo. They use a collaborative process for analyzing and solving problems, and have the ability to adjust to ever-changing environmental conditions. Effective leaders possess a keen awareness of stakeholder needs and expectations. Most important, they build synergistic relationships with their employees, which stimulate them to achieve personal and organizational excellence.

Employees cannot become the organization's greatest asset without effective leadership because organizational leaders provide the vision, insight, intuition, and power to effect organizational transformation. Their collective intellectual capabilities are required to create a developmental environment that treats employees as the resource of greatest value. By improving their self-reflective, strategic thinking, interpersonal, and performance-enhancing skills, leaders are in an excellent position to traverse the performance abyss.

Chapter 10

CREATING VIRTUAL TEAMS

Another important strategy that organizations can use to address the performance challenge is to make the transformation from work groups to virtual teams. In this way, organizations generate collaborative solutions to complex performance problems, ones that are addressed by the individuals most qualified to resolve them—employees.

Organizations have been examining ways of developing and improving teams for more than twenty years. One problem is that organizations do a poor job of defining and effectively creating teams. Several questions need to be addressed when considering these issues:

- What is a work group?
- What is a performance team?
- What is a virtual team?
- What is the difference between a work group and a performance team?
- What is the difference between a performance team and a virtual team?
- How can we develop healthy teams that meet organizational goals and objectives?

In this chapter, we will address these questions and examine the similarities and differences among work groups, performance teams, and virtual teams, how different individuals (managers, performance coaches, and leaders) influence each of the respective entities, and how they are linked to the organization's business strategy (Figure 10.1). We will start by examining business strategy and its relationship to work groups, performance teams, and virtual teams.

BUSINESS STRATEGY

Very few employees work independently of the organization's business strategy. To do so threatens their job security. Business strategy is the way in which an organization plans to remain financially stable and viable. Stability is maintenance of an organization's profitability and consistent return on stakeholders' investments. Viability is the organization's ability to survive, the results of successful long-term planning, growth, and profitability.

When we discussed the job design process (Chapter 3), we stressed that every employee needs to understand how he or she impacts, links, and aligns himself or herself to the organization's strategic business goals and objectives. The same thing must occur for work groups, performance teams, and virtual teams. These three entities must identify the assignments that help them produce performance outputs and activities that are directly linked to the organization's business strategy. If they are not identified, organizations waste valuable human and financial resources.

WORK GROUPS

A work group is a group of individuals whose jobs are to fulfill a specific performance task (Figure 10.1). Such groups have a specific goal to accomplish although members can work independently in achieving the goal. Most commonly, a number of individuals are doing the same task with very little interaction among members. Furthermore, few members are involved in the decision-making process. When problems arise, individual members rely on their manager or supervisor for resolution. Sometimes more experienced work group members are asked to help resolve outstanding issues.

Work groups focus on a single task, troubleshooting and resolving problems related to it. One of the best examples of a work group is a customer service center where hundreds of individuals answer telephone calls and are responsible for addressing customer problems and requests. Customer service representatives' performance is measured by the volume of calls handled and the number of successful resolutions achieved. Customer service representatives work independently of their peers regardless of their proximity. Some customer service departments nominally reward their employees for their combined efforts; however, these rewards rarely build a team concept because employees do not work collectively to achieve performance outputs.

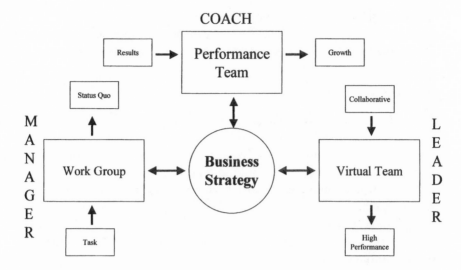

Figure 10.1 Team-building Process

Work groups, by virtue of focusing on specific tasks, assume the responsibility of making sure that performance problems are resolved in such a way as to preserve and maintain the financial stability of the organization as well as the quality of problem solving. If work groups are unsuccessful in meeting the needs and expectations of their stakeholders, both internal and external, the organization will suffer financially. This is one of the reasons why it is so important that work groups meet rigid, precise performance standards (see Chapter 3). We are not suggesting that work groups are totally one-dimensional, focusing on only a singular task or maintaining performance status quo. On the contrary, work groups need to constantly develop their employees. A continuous developmental approach permits each work group member to provide input into changes that streamline and create the necessary efficiencies required for total quality management. Work group members possess a great capacity for intellectual curiosity, which if used appropriately fuels rapid and dramatic change within an organization.

Most organizations that use work groups do not subscribe to an inclusive or developmental philosophy. They treat members of work groups as a means to an end. In other words, organizations want their employees to simply do the jobs assigned to them. If they do not perform the task correctly, they are simply replaced by other employees.

Many organizations do a poor job of valuing the worth of work groups, as they fail to establish ways that members can measure their performance quality and contributions. They do not inspire, motivate, or energize members to improve their performance or encourage their input.

Managers

Managers are most closely associated with work groups because their primary responsibilities are to supervise workflow, assign work assignments, and oversee production. Work group managers enhance performance by making certain that each employee fulfills his or her respective job responsibilities, completes performance tasks, and produces performance outputs.

We asked a number of individuals from a variety of organizations to describe the term "manager." The most often identified characteristics or descriptors were:

- task-oriented
- director of employee activities
- supervisor
- workflow coordinator
- motivator
- work performance critic

These characteristics or descriptors reflect the directive and autocratic nature of the manager role, which is reflected in the type of role responsibilities most managers have within their organizations.

Because work groups are only focused on singular tasks or the maintenance of current performance levels, managers are used as shepherds of employee performance. Thus, they have difficulty generating thought-provoking discussions that produce improved business results. Consequently, work groups limit organizational growth and expansion opportunities, which is the primary reason organizations should adopt a performance team or virtual team approach.

PERFORMANCE TEAMS

Performance teams increase the performance capacity of organizations by focusing on achieving business results (work groups focus only on task completion). This difference in focus is what separates performance teams from work groups. Performance teams are assembled to produce results or a positive "win/loss record" for the organization. Wins come in many forms, such as increased market share, improved quality, better on-time delivery, enhanced customer service, and so on. Performance teams focus on achieving results that demonstrate a winning tradition.

Another fundamental difference between work groups and performance teams is that performance teams are assembled to discover creative ways of improving productivity, which in turn provides employees with growth and development opportunities. This occurs because performance teams are put together to achieve success through results while work groups are responsible for simply executing tasks. This difference is paramount in creating a developmental philosophy within the organization. Consequently, performance teams must always provide members with opportunities to build on their strengths through delegating and partnering activities (see Chapter 8).

According to Katzenbach and Smith (1994), a performance team is a small number of people with complementary skills who are committed to a common purpose, performance goals, and approach for which they hold themselves mutually accountable. These six elements define the size, membership requirements, outcomes, strategies, and evaluation process of performance teams.

Because performance teams are assembled to achieve specific, well-defined objectives (business results) they must have clearly defined roles and identified performance activities to follow (Larson & LaFasto, 1989). Each team member must depend on his or her colleagues to perform their jobs to exact performance standards, thus producing performance outputs that meet or exceed standards and are delivered on time. Otherwise performance objectives are jeopardized. Therefore, performance teams are characterized by *clarity*.

Once a performance team's purpose has been determined, it is important to design teams so they can function effectively. Larson and LaFasto (1989) identified four distinctive features of such teams:

1. clear roles, responsibilities, and accountabilities
2. an effective communication system that ensures that information is easily accessible, creditable, and documentable
3. methods for monitoring individual performance and providing feedback
4. an emphasis on fact-based judgments (p. 55)

Each of these features varies from performance team to performance team, depending on their emphasis and purpose.

When assembling performance teams, Williams (1997) believes that coachable people must be chosen to avoid unnecessary conflicts and to help create an atmosphere of continuous improvement. He believes that performance teams should remain together until they complete their assignments and responsibilities because *turnover* is a team killer. He advocates that team members should help each other develop their respective skills and abilities and reinforce each other emotionally and spiritually. When these elements are present in performance teams, exceptional business results and outcomes are produced.

Assembling coachable team members is only one way of ensuring their success. Team members also must work effectively together. Williams (1997) contends that performance teams should be well balanced, consisting of the most talented employees capable of creating "synergistic chemistry" within the team. High performance will be the result of this type of chemistry and teamwork.

We believe that there are several characteristics that foster chemistry and teamwork. They include:

C = character—doing the right thing when no one else is looking.
H = humanism—looking for positive attributes in every team member.
E = empathy—understanding another perspective and point of view.
M = motivation—demonstrating internal desire to succeed.
I = initiative—performing above and beyond expectations.
S = supportive—encouraging risk taking and innovation.
T = togetherness—working as one to achieve a common goal.
R = responsible—owning one's efforts and decisions.
Y = yielding—compromising when appropriate.

T = trust—accepting and believing in individual team members.
E = equality—allowing separate but equal roles.
A = adaptability—adjusting to ever-changing conditions and situations.
M = maturity—dealing with difficult problems in an appropriate way.
W = winning attitude—expecting to achieve positive results.
O = organized—using effective and efficient work plans.
R = respect—accepting individual differences, approaches, and abilities.
K = kindred spirit—possessing a common oneness.

When these seventeen characteristics are present, performance teams will achieve great success.

Performance teams create an energy that, when channeled appropriately, can lead to incredible results. It is important to understand that performance teams evolve through four distinct phases of development. Each phase must be carefully managed to ensure healthy matriculation to the next level. The phases are:

1. Forming—where initial group interaction occurs and ground rules for behavior and achievement are discussed.
2. Storming—where team members express conflicts of interest and needs openly in order to create leadership positions, influence, and control.
3. Norming—where rules are established and team members accept one another, create interpersonal bonds, and accept their respective roles among the group.
4. Performing—where high performance and desired business results are achieved because of the total contributions of every member of the team.

One of the outcomes of performance teams is growth and development opportunities that create a synergistic partnership between employees and the organization. Furthermore, growth and development opportunities help employees improve their performance and productivity while helping the organization improve its profitability, revenue growth, and quality. As these occur the organization will have more financial resources to invest in its people. Such a process produces an infinite cycle of continuous growth and development.

Heterogeneous Performance Teams

Team members provide each other with growth and development opportunities by challenging thoughts, ideas, creations, and efforts, which can lead to better business results. These growth and development opportunities can be seized with greater success by creating heterogeneous performance teams rather than homogeneous ones.

Heterogeneous teams consist of individuals with very different backgrounds, experiences, demographic histories, values, beliefs, and performance orientations. Members come from all vantage points and tend to be challengers. Heterogeneous performance teams tend to have extremely lively debates over issues and ideas, resulting in vast amounts of information being exchanged. Sometimes strong-willed individuals dominate the interaction and attempt to force their beliefs on others, which can negatively impact working relationships. If managed appropriately, however, such discussions provide an organization with a greater opportunity for success as well-tested and challenged thoughts, ideas, and actions surface. Thus, the *positive tension* required of long-lasting and continuous growth and development emerges.

By comparison, homogeneous performance teams consist of "like-minded" individuals with similar backgrounds, experiences, demographic histories, values, beliefs, and performance orientations. Not surprisingly, members of such groups tend to get along very well with each other and agree quickly, yet fail to generate discussions that produce new, dramatic insights and revelations. Consequently, homogeneous performance teams do not provide the *positive tension* required for substantial growth and development.

Performance Coaches

Performance teams focus on different outcomes than work groups; thus, they require a different type of supervision. The most effective type of supervisor is a performance coach, who is more results-oriented than a manager (see Chapter 5). Performance coaches differ from managers in several other ways, as demonstrated by comparing their respective characteristics and descriptors. The same audience used previously stated that performance coaches are characterized as:

- achievers
- accomplishers
- bold
- charismatic
- motivators
- leaders
- challengers
- counselors
- commitment builders
- confronters
- developers
- trainers

Upon examination, our small group of respondents has a more positive perception of performance coaches than of managers. In fact, a common theme emerges for performance coaches in that they are simultaneously results-oriented and people-oriented. As a result, employees are much more likely to work harmoniously with performance coaches than with managers. Our group believes that performance coaches tend to have a higher degree of energy, enthusiasm, and passion than do managers. In short, performance coaches are more effective than managers at motivating their employees (team members) to achieve desired business results.

VIRTUAL TEAMS

In some organizations the tension between employees and management severely retards organizational efficiency and productivity. This tension can be caused by the organizational structure, the work climate, or poor interpersonal relationships between managers and employees. Often, organizations believe that if the energy spent trying to reduce this tension could be captured, it could be applied to more profitable areas. Furthermore, no one person can generate the kind of dynamic energy, ideas, or actions needed to address all the problems facing today's organizations. Thus, it is inherently in an organization's best interest to use the collective intelligence of many individuals to address their problems. One way of harnessing the synergistic abilities of an organization to reduce tension and to analyze and solve problems is to develop virtual teams.

Virtual teams are small groups of people, usually four to twelve in number, who do similar work, meet regularly to identify and analyze organizational and performance problems in their areas, recommend their solutions to management, and implement the solution approved by management. This approach recognizes the importance of employees in the problem-solving effort, and emphasizes their collaborative and creative nature.

Larson and LaFasto (1989) believe that the primary purpose of virtual teams is to resolve job-related problems. As a result, virtual teams are responsible for exploring possibilities and alternatives that require a tremendous amount of autonomy and freedom to function successfully. In addition, each team member must believe that fellow team members are being truthful and demonstrating a high degree of integrity during interactions. Team members must value and respect each other for their ideas, commitment, and contributions to guarantee the success of virtual teams. These elements become the distinguishing characteristic of virtual teams. Larson and LaFasto (1989) believe that these characteristics:

1. allow team members to remain problem-focused.
2. promote more effective communications and coordination.

3. improve the quality of collaborative outcomes.
4. lead to compensating work styles, where one team member picks up the slack that occurs when another member falters (pp. 88–92).

Managers and executives do not have a monopoly on ideas and thoughts. As a result, virtual teams are based on the premise that the people who do a job understand it well and are best equipped to improve the quality of their work. Virtual teams allow employees to resolve many of the problems that negatively impact day-to-day operations. They are a participatory management tool designed to systematically harness the brain power of employees to solve organizational problems of productivity and quality. Virtual teams are behaviorally based and represent management's awareness that employees can positively contribute to an organization. They demonstrate the importance of human resources by inviting participation.

Virtual teams are results-oriented, but are also concerned with the development of people. According to Gilley (1985), employees want dignity; they want the human element, the people-building concept, put back in the workplace. This people-building philosophy is demonstrated through management's sincere efforts to provide challenging problems for employees to solve.

There are four cardinal principles of virtual teams. First, team members are granted the autonomy and freedom to decide which problem(s) they will address, allowing members the opportunity *to support what they create*. Second, virtual teams bring decision making closer to those who actually do the job, thereby allowing members to communicate to management what they feel are the solutions to problems facing the organization. Third, virtual teams are based on the concept of collective-collaborative problem solving, where team members strive to create win-win solutions to difficult organizational problems. Collective-collaborative problem solving was discussed in Chapter 5 and is a proven approach that allows for both employee and management input and involvement. Fourth, virtual teams are based on trust.

Virtual teams have several elements, characteristics, and procedures that are essential to their success. The elements include a group leader, voluntary group participation, brainstorming as a way of generating solutions, collaborative problem solving, data gathering, decision analysis, written documentation of decisions and actions, and record keeping. The essential characteristics include top-level management support and sponsorship, problem solving at lower levels, recognition of participants, and rewarding accomplishments. Virtual team procedures include establishing lines of accountability, training at all levels, long-range planning, inviting participation and the evaluation of results.

As a way of assuring success, virtual team members are expected to:

1. Demonstrate a realistic understanding of their roles and accountabilities.
2. Demonstrate objective and fact-based judgments.
3. Collaborate effectively with other team members.
4. Make the team goal a higher priority than any personal objective.
5. Demonstrate a willingness to devote whatever effort is necessary to achieve team success.
6. Be willing to share information, perceptions, and feedback openly.
7. Provide help to other team members when needed and appropriate.
8. Demonstrate high standards of excellence.
9. Stand behind and support team decisions.
10. Demonstrate courage of conviction by directly confronting important issues.
11. Demonstrate leadership in ways that contribute to the team's success.
12. Respond constructively to feedback from others (Larson & LaFasto, 1989, p. 124).

These twelve principles place the responsibility for appropriate team behavior squarely on the shoulders of team members, requiring each person to be cooperative and collaborative.

Leaders

Work groups have managers, performance teams have performance coaches, and virtual teams have leaders. As discussed in Chapter 9, critical reflectivity, strategic thinking, performance enhancement, and interpersonal relationship competencies of effective leaders are applied to virtual teams to obtain positive results and to provide development opportunities for members.

According to our group of respondents, leaders possess the following characteristics:

- charismatic
- gregarious
- energetic
- inspiring
- supportive
- decisive
- visionary

These individuals address the most difficult issues and problems that plague an organization with confidence and courage.

Employees have a clear understanding of the problems that exist within their organization. As information flows up, organization filters are in place that allow less and less information to make it to leaders at the top. We have found that upper management usually hears less than 5 percent of the problems that exist within the organization (Figure 10.2).

The exact opposite occurs when the triangle is inverted and the focus is on the decision-making process (Figure 10.2). The vast majority of decisions are made by the organization's leaders while the more menial decisions are made at the bottom of the organization. Consequently, workers (employees) rarely make any job-related decisions at all. In some organizations, they are treated like second-class citizens who don't have a clue about how products are made or services are delivered. This is a monumental mistake in organizations.

As a way of improving the quality of virtual teams, team leaders should:

1. Avoid compromising the team's objectives with political issues.
2. Exhibit personal commitment to the team's goal.
3. Not dilute the team's efforts with too many priorities.
4. Be fair and impartial toward all team members.
5. Be willing to confront and resolve issues associated with inadequate performance by team members.
6. Be open to new ideas and information from team members (Larson & LaFasto, 1989, p. 123).

Leaders who demonstrate these characteristics are dedicated to the overall success of the team as well as each individual member. Integrating these ideas enables leaders to adhere to a set of guiding principles that reflect the importance of cooperation, collaboration, teamwork, and respect for people.

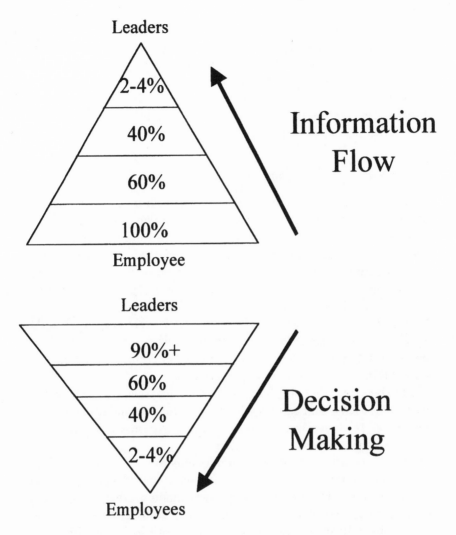

Figure 10.2 Information and Decision Making in Organizations

HARMONY AND EFFICIENCY MODEL OF VIRTUAL TEAMS

The concept of virtual teams is based on the assumption that employees possess a greater knowledge of job-related problems because they perform job tasks on a regular basis and thus are familiar with the components of each job. Leaders, on the other hand, have the authority to solve job-related problems and are in a position to exercise control and change related to each job.

Virtual teams have two fundamental goals. One is to increase organizational leaders' knowledge of job-related problems. Another is to increase the employees' authority to solve job-related problems.

Based on the assumptions and goals of virtual teams, it is possible to construct a model that reveals their relationships. In addition, a model illustrates the increased effectiveness of leaders and employees working together to resolve organizational problems.

Assumptions of Virtual Teams

The virtual team's assumptions can be illustrated by constructing two continuums, one horizontal and one vertical. The horizontal continuum reveals the level of knowledge one has of job-related problems. The vertical continuum reveals the level of authority one has to solve job-related problems.

By combining the two continuums, the basic assumptions of virtual teams can be diagrammed (Figure 10.3). For comparison, employees are placed along the horizontal axis while leaders are positioned at the top of the vertical axis. In addition, a numerical scale is assigned to both axes, where 10 represents a high level and 1 represents a low level. This scale will be used to illustrate the model's use.

For demonstration purposes, it is necessary to select arbitrary values for the knowledge and authority levels of employees and leaders. In reality, these levels will vary according to the experience of employees and the organizational level of leaders.

The dynamics of the various components previously described are better understood when presented in a comprehensive model (Figure 10.3). As the model indicates, employees retain a greater knowledge level of job-related issues while leaders retain a higher level of authority to solve job-related problems, regardless of the number of virtual teams developed. This condition exists because employees maintain constant contact with performance activities that are used to produce performance outputs. On the other hand, leaders retain their level of authority, which they are reluctant to relinquish even when virtual teams are used.

To illustrate, consider the following example. Employees on the horizontal axis have a high degree of knowledge of job-related problems (9) but lack the authority to solve them (3). In addition, leaders at this level on the vertical axis have a high level of authority (9) but a low level of knowledge concerning job-related problems (3) (Figure 10.4).

The shaded area in the lower left-hand corner represents the area of

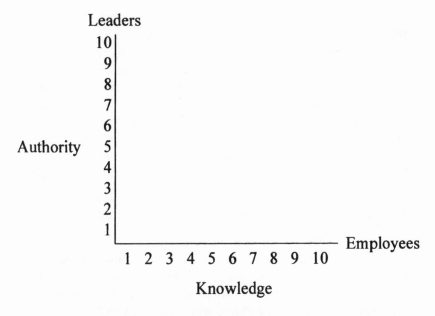

Figure 10.3 Harmony and Efficiency Model

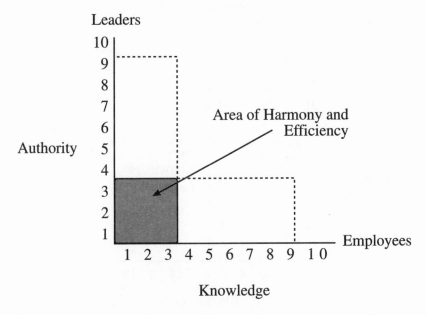

Figure 10.4 Comparing Leaders' and Employees' Knowledge of Job-related Problems and Authority to Solve Job-related Problems (Gilley & Galbraith, 1984)

congruence between employees' and leaders' knowledge of job-related problems and their authority to solve them. According to Gilley and Galbraith (1984), this intersection is referred to as the area of harmony and efficiency (Figure 10.4). In this area, leaders and employees function in harmony because their respective levels of authority and knowledge of job-related problems are equal. These modest levels of authority and knowledge (3,3) allow leaders and employees to address minor performance problems (which is their level of efficiency). Efficiency is, however, limited because employees lack the level of authority to solve job-related problems while leaders lack knowledge of these problems.

Achieving the Goals of Virtual Teams

Virtual teams utilize the collective knowledge of employees, enabling communication of their perceptions of problem solutions to organizational leaders. As virtual team members identify organizational problems and possible solutions, leaders become more aware of the components that comprise performance activities and job-related problems. This increases leaders' knowledge of job-related problems, which represents the first goal of virtual teams (Figure 10.5). In our example, leaders' knowledge of job-related problems increased from 3 to 6.

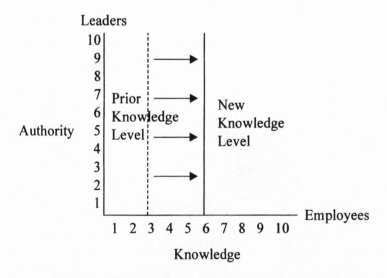

Figure 10.5 Increasing Leaders' Knowledge of Job-related Problems (Gilley & Galbraith, 1984).

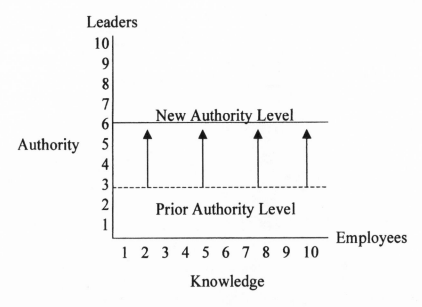

Figure 10.6 Increasing Employees' Authority to Solve Job-related Problems (Gilley & Galbraith, 1984).

Simultaneously, virtual team members obtain vital experiences by participating in organizational decision-making activities and are given opportunities to propose changes in the organization's operations. In return, leaders develop confidence in members' abilities to make decisions and begin to view them as practical, contributing, productive, and dedicated employees. As this situation perpetuates itself, leaders develop a more positive attitude toward virtual team members, and are more inclined to allow them to obtain higher levels of authority. Thus, the second goal of virtual teams, which is to increase employees' level of authority to solve job-related problems, is achieved. In Figure 10.6, the employees' authority to solve job-related problems has increased from 3 to 6.

Increasing leaders' knowledge of job-related problems and increasing employees' authority to solve problems produces a higher level of harmony and efficiency. The increased harmony between leaders and employees improves their collective problem-solving effectiveness, which in turn improves the efficiency of the organization because leaders are more aware of job-related problems and effectively address them. On the other hand, employees are free to respond to job-related problems more quickly because they have been granted greater decision-making latitude by the organization (Figure 10.7).

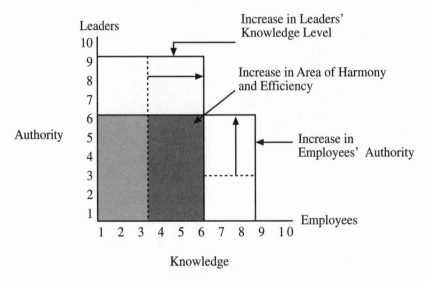

Figure 10.7 Increasing Areas of Harmony and Efficiency (Gilley & Galbraith, 1984).

If leaders were omniscient concerning job-related problems and employees were omnipotent concerning authority to exercise change in an organization, then virtual teams would have no utility. However, neither circumstance is a current reality in most organizations.

The relationship between leaders' and employees' knowledge of job-related problems and authority to solve problems can be modeled. The comprehensive model illustrates the fundamental goals of virtual teams, which are to increase leaders' knowledge of job-related problems and to increase employees' level of authority to solve problems. The successful alignment of these two goals results in a more harmonious and efficient organization (Figure 10.7). Finally, it reveals the importance of increasing the area of harmony and efficiency in any organization, which leads to increased productivity and profitability.

To achieve a higher level of harmony and efficiency, leaders must encourage risk taking on the part of team members (employees) by providing a supportive decision-making climate. Leaders can provide this climate by:

1. Trusting team members with meaningful levels of responsibility.
2. Providing team members with the necessary autonomy to achieve results.

3. Presenting challenging opportunities that stretch the individual abilities of team members.
4. Recognizing and rewarding superior performance.
5. Standing behind the team and supporting it (Larson & LaFasto, 1989, p. 126).

When these behaviors are present, virtual team members will be encouraged to unleash their talents and abilities, resulting in effective, efficient decisions and outcomes.

CONCLUSION

By successfully and appropriately using work groups, performance teams, and virtual teams, an organization will develop a practical strategy that addresses the performance challenge. To this end, organizations benefit by improving their decision-making capacity, enhancing employee commitment and involvement, increasing organizational collaboration and cooperation, and providing performance growth and development opportunities for employees.

Chapter 11

BEYOND THE LEARNING ORGANIZATION

Most organizations claim that their customers are their number one priority, asserting that all of their energies, efforts, and resources are focused on customer satisfaction. While certainly a noble strategy—and we strongly concur with the notion of meeting or exceeding customer expectations—this emphasis is misguided. We believe that an organization's greatest asset is its employees—who should be the firm's number one focus. No organization is capable of superior customer satisfaction without hard-working, dedicated employees who adhere to and strongly believe in their vision and mission (Carlson, 1987). Employees tend to treat customers the way they themselves are treated. Poor treatment begets the same. Those treated with dignity, honesty, concern, and respect pass this on to customers, resulting in improved employee–customer relations and satisfaction. It is impossible to address the performance challenge without an organization's willingness to examine its philosophy toward employees.

Over the past decade a philosophical shift has occurred through acceptance of the learning organization. Many are touting its methods, advantages, and benefits, having concluded that the learning organization is the answer to organizational change and development. We agree that learning is a prerequisite to development, and that it makes sense to focus on the aspects, principles, and policies required to transform a traditional organization into a learning organization. However, we refuse to accept the notion that the learning organization represents the evolutionary pinnacle of organizational transformation.

We believe that the next evolutionary step in organizational life is to that of a *developmental organization*. A developmental organization focuses all of its energy and resources on enhancing the collective talent of its employees for the purpose of better serving customers in an efficient, effective manner. Ours is a strongly focused philosophical shift that must be made if organizations plan to continue the long, challenging journey toward organizational success.

190

The transformation from traditional or learning organization into a developmental organization is as much philosophical as pragmatic. In developmental organizations, leaders philosophically recognize that members of the entire organization must be involved in the realization of its mission, vision, and goals for all to enjoy prosperity. Pragmatically, developmental organizations will not be successful unless leaders, managers, supervisors, and employees collectively blend their talents toward achievement of strategic business goals and objectives. Improper treatment and utilization of human resources inhibits performance outputs. Organizational efficiency and effectiveness cannot be achieved without enhancing the skills, expertise, talents, and intellectual capital of all organizational members.

Creating a developmental organization involves seven activities critical to success:

1. Reinventing the human resource department.
2. Linking employee performance goals to the organization's strategic business goals and objectives.
3. Adopting an inclusive approach to organizational problem solving.
4. Incorporating diversity into the fabric of the organization.
5. Embracing career development strategies.
6. Adopting a continuous change philosophy.
7. Overcoming the self-defeating behaviors of dysfunctional organizations.

These stand-alone strategies combine to form a strong game plan by which organizations can transform themselves into developmental organizations.

REINVENTING HUMAN RESOURCES: BLESSING OR BURDEN?

As organizations consider strategies for addressing the performance challenge as well as creating a developmental organization philosophy, one important department, human resources (HR), must be examined closely to determine its role and relationships. Traditionally, this department is responsible for compensation and benefits, training and development, and performance management. Typically, the HR department consists of specialists in each of these areas responsible for their narrow area of expertise.

It should come as no surprise that HR departments suffer from an image problem. In many organizations HR departments are not considered major players. Sadly, in many cases they have become "the proverbial Rodney Dangerfield of the organization, receiving little or none of the respect they deserve" (Flannery, Hofrichter, & Platten, 1996, p. 106). Due to this lack of respect, many HR professionals suffer from low self-esteem and a persecution complex. Consequently, many HR professionals find themselves in a quandary: do they maintain their narrow, specialized focus, or do they become strategic partners within the organization?

Flannery, Hofrichter, and Platten (1996) have concluded that the traditional HR department is frequently a major barrier to the development of new processes and procedures designed to improve an organization's efficiency and effectiveness. Therefore, it is essential that HR departments shift from their traditional, narrowly focused, and confining boxes to a more integrated and strategic alignment. Gilley and Maycunich (1998) refer to this evolution of the HR department as *strategic integration*—a concept based on the belief that human resource departments should not be organized as separate operational entities, but should be free-flowing functions within the organization. They contend that traditional HR departments should be broken down into operationally attached HR functions, thereby helping units, departments, and divisions discover ways of addressing the performance challenge such that employees become the organization's greatest asset. HR professionals should also become internally customer-focused, helping managers and supervisors lead, direct, coach, and reward their employees.

Two critical questions must be answered by HR professionals prior to preparing a customer service response:

- Why does demand differ for HR interventions and consulting services?
- What type of customer service response is appropriate for differing demand states?

To answer these questions, HR professionals must understand the characteristics of differing demand states and the correct customer service response for each.

Several factors help HR professionals determine the demand states facing their clients, including: (1) interest in and need for a specific intervention or consulting service, (2) the credibility of HR within the organization, (3) the financial condition of the organization, (4) the organization's cultural climate, (5) managers' and employees' attitudes toward HR interventions and consulting services, and (6) managers' and employees' previous experience with HR departments, their professionals, interventions, and services (Gilley & Maycunich, 1998). Once these factors have been identified, HR professionals should use the information as a baseline, allowing them to be responsive yet responsible when addressing internal customers' requests.

In order to improve their credibility, HR professionals must be willing to leave the "mother ship"—their highly centralized administrative units—and become fully integrated into the broader business operations (Gilley & Maycunich, 1998). As a result, managers should handle the majority of training and development responsibilities formerly assigned to HR professionals (see Chapter 5). In addition, managers should become more actively involved in the selection, recruiting, and hiring of new employees. HR professionals, in return, should be willing to share their compensation and reward responsibilities with managers and supervisors (Flannery, Hofrichter, & Platten, 1996).

When the idea of strategically integrating HR into the organization is first proposed, many HR professionals become quite defensive. Some spend a great deal of time and energy attempting to block the evolution. The primary reason for resistance is that HR professionals perceive loss of both position and power when many of their current duties are delegated or shared with managers and supervisors. Fortunately, just the opposite is true. Rather than continuing the role of administrative housekeepers and organizational bit players, HR professionals, if fully utilized, become key strategists in the business process.

Gilley and Maycunich (1998) contend that HR professionals have the responsibility to think like other business people within the organization to demonstrate their credibility and value. In this way, they will be viewed as equal business partners within the organization. However, if HR professionals "refuse to budge and cling tenaciously to the traditional structures and strategies, they will be seen as part of the problem and will be indeed left out of the process" (Flannery, Hofrichter, & Platten, 1996, p. 208).

Human resource professionals help organizations address the performance challenge and simultaneously help them become developmental by working closely with managers and providing a full range of performance alignment activities. They include:

- designing jobs and workflow
- selecting and recruiting employees

- developing employees
- measuring and managing performance
- helping managers make the transition to performance coaching
- transforming performance appraisals into developmental evaluations
- helping managers and employees create performance growth and development plans
- linking compensation and rewards to performance growth and development

In short, HR professionals help their organizations become developmentally focused, transforming their employees into their greatest asset.

LINKING EMPLOYEE PERFORMANCE GOALS TO STRATEGIC BUSINESS GOALS AND OBJECTIVES

One of the biggest mistakes an organization makes is failure to link all employees to its strategic business goals and objectives. As we have discussed previously, competency maps are critical to organizational success (see Chapter 3), providing the framework with which to identify skills, knowledge, and attitudes necessary for business success. Unfortunately, this is where most organizational efforts stop because they feel developing employee competencies translates into financial success. While partially true, employees need specific targets by which to focus their energies, efforts, and competencies. The perfect target is the organization's strategic business goals and objectives. In this way, all eyes are directed on the outcomes most critical to organizational stability, growth, and success.

We believe that an organization needs to change its approach by communicating its goals and objectives to every employee (Figure 11.1). An educated workforce understands how it impacts and improves business results that owners or shareholders expect and demand. Furthermore, an educated workforce is fundamental to driving organizational success, an approach that needs to be the foundation of the developmental organization.

The easiest way to accomplish this in an organization is to openly discuss the business plan, including how each employee ultimately impacts and affects organizational ability to achieve desired goals and objectives. This approach should be initiated at the highest level within the organization.

Strategic Business Goals
and Objectives

CEO
Team

Executives

Midlevel Managers

Front-Line Supervisors

Front-Line Employees

Communicating Goals

Linking to Goals

Figure 11.1 Employee Linkage to Business Goals

Strategic business goals and objectives need to be specific, measurable, yet realistic. They need to be macro so that business units, departments, and divisions can break them down into more manageable components and incorporate them into their individual and team goals. The responsibility here lies on all levels of leadership, from executive to supervisory.

To ensure that all employees focus on appropriate results, it is critical that everyone throughout the organization clearly understands the organization's strategic business goals and objectives. By focusing on business results, employees will feel more like owners and participate accordingly.

In Chapter 10 we discussed the importance of virtual teams and their impact on the organization, and illustrated the power of employee participation in designing organizational strategy. We discussed the value of employee participation in the decision-making process, which increases their understanding of the intricacies of organizational operations and their personal impact on results—so critical to organizational success. The vast majority of employees want to work each day feeling valued and challenged, but, most important, they want to be contributing members to the successful operation of their organization.

ADOPTING AN INCLUSIVE APPROACH TO ORGANIZATIONAL PROBLEM SOLVING

Organizations too often do an absolutely miserable job of meeting the needs of their employees. Shortsighted, misguided leaders and managers act as taskmasters, believing that employees are simply responsible for routinely doing their jobs. Rarely are employees credited for being thinking, creative human beings. Executives throughout the business world focus on employee seclusion, truly believing that employees have no concern for the business's financial aspects. Thus they require no exposure to the competitive business environment. This protective attitude is extremely detrimental to the organization, and may have a negative ripple effect throughout the entire business.

Seclusion is a monster waiting to attack. Excluding employees from the decision-making process fosters mediocrity, as they will focus on simply getting the job done and not creatively, collaboratively solving problems. Taking the inclusive approach to organizational effectiveness provides the foundation for continued and future development. Inclusion is simply listening to and acting on issues raised by employees at all levels of the organization (see Chapter 10).

Leaders and managers must take heed: employee experience is not a criterion for listening. Focusing only on those employees possessing vast amounts of experience merely supports the status quo. Employees new to the workforce or organization offer fresh perspectives unprejudiced by the organization's internal political machine. Lack of bias allows new organizational members to provide information useful in overcoming inertia and pushing the firm to greater heights. New employees require delicate treatment due to their fear of being labeled or associated with certain groups. Their safety must be assured prior to sustaining a comfort level that encourages honest exchange of ideas and information relevant to organizational issues. Listening and valuing new employee knowledge goes a long way toward developing synergistic relationships.

Inclusion can occur at all levels within an organization. One of the most formidable tools and processes that encourages inclusion is virtual teaming, discussed in detail in Chapter 10. Inclusion's underlying premise is that employees are knowledgeable about job-related problems and, if granted the authority to solve them, will greatly improve the overall harmony and efficiency of the organization. This valuable strategy fosters developmental organizations.

INCORPORATING DIVERSITY INTO THE FABRIC OF THE ORGANIZATION

Knowledge cannot be limited to job specifics. Diversity must be discussed in macro terms that include every element of demographic makeup. This includes but is not limited to the following:

- gender
- ethnicity
- education
- work experience
- sexual orientation
- religion
- income
- special needs

Building diversity into the fabric of the organization enables creation of a tolerant workforce accepting of each other's respective differences while still challenging one another and demanding excellence.

Organizations have wasted millions of dollars on improperly executed diversity programs that have failed to impact effectiveness. The key is to take an inclusive approach, addressing diversity with open, honest discussions on issues involving fear in the workplace (e.g., AIDS and other socially transmitted diseases). Diversity needs to become the cornerstone of every business.

We have previously discussed heterogeneous teams and would like to take this topic further. Creating an environment that encourages and supports heterogeneous teams fosters the opportunity for growth of diversity as well. What do we mean? Work groups, performance teams, and virtual teams can provide the fabric to create an organization's own patchwork quilt based on the diversity of the workforce. These entities can turn the oft-maligned procedural manual characteristic of diversity programs into powerful, impactful reality. Creation of heterogeneous teams allows managers to implement and practice the spirit of the manual's written words rather than express the continuous platitudes so common in diversity programs.

EMBRACING CAREER DEVELOPMENT STRATEGIES

Career development is a critical strategy used in creating developmental organizations. Most performance and organizational problems are career-related; employees often feel trapped, stagnated, or overlooked in their present jobs or occupations (Gilley & Eggland, 1989). Many employees derive little pleasure from their current jobs, which contributes to ever-increasing stress and lower performance outputs. These employees do not work up to their full potential, often failing to meet organizational expectations. Many have lost their occupational mission in life or have been unable to identify their vocational purpose.

Career development programs provide a more systematic approach to reducing organizational and performance problems. They allow and encourage employees to examine their future career plans and analyze their abilities and interests to better match their personal growth and development needs with those of the organization. For their part, organizations can increase productivity, improve employee attitudes, and develop greater worker satisfaction and loyalty by adopting this developmental strategy. As a way of reducing organizational performance problems, career development promotes a more efficient allocation of human resources and greater loyalty among workers.

Career development, as a developmental strategy, is an organized, planned effort comprised of structured activities and processes that result in the mutual development of employees and organizations. This strategy includes both career planning and career management.

Organizations implement career development programs in order to:

1. develop and promote employees
2. reduce turnover
3. create a developmental philosophy
4. maintain an appropriate stream of talented, dedicated employees
5. improve organizational effectiveness and efficiency
6. develop a collaborative, synergistic work environment dedicated to the delivery of quality products and services

Career development programs communicate strong employee interests, which can be advantageous in improving the organization's image and ultimately reposition the organization in the marketplace.

Organizations cannot and will not develop employees adequately unless they offer challenging career development activities. Top management must develop an appropriate awareness and appreciation of this developmental strategy, actively participating in identification and design of challenging assignments. Absent upper management support and involvement, career development will continue to proceed in piecemeal fashion, if at all.

Effective career development programs focus on long-term results and account for the diversity of people, using methods other than the traditional training and development approach. Suggested alternatives include mentoring, virtual teaming, self-directed learning and development projects, adoption of performance growth and development plans throughout the organization, and appointing employees to participate in challenging projects and work activities that further their growth and development.

In career development, employees are responsible for career planning while the organization is answerable for career management. According to Gilley and Eggland (1989), career planning is a process of setting up employees' career objectives and developing activities that will achieve them. They contend that career management entails specific human resource activities such as developmental evaluations, training, mentoring, education, and human resource planning, which guarantees that the organization has the correct number and appropriate types of employees in the right jobs at all times. These two processes comprise a system of *organizational career development* that serves as a framework on which organizations design future developmental approaches.

Human Resource Planning

Human resource planning is the major component of career management activities within an organization. A shortage of experienced, talented human resources increases the need for long-term human resource planning actions. Organizations must engage in developmental planning based on their goals and objectives, and properly allocate human resources accordingly.

Human resource planning is viewed as a process, not merely as part of the HR staff's daily activities. The process involves analyzing an organization's human resource needs under changing conditions and developing the strategy necessary to satisfy these long-term needs. From this perspective human resource planning is a two-step process consisting of needs forecasting and program planning. With the analysis of needs, priorities can be determined and human resources allocated to satisfy existing and future needs via the entire performance alignment process. By ascertaining future human resources required and future human resources available the organization can determine and plan for surpluses or deficiencies.

Career Planning

Career planning can be seen as a personal process consisting of *developmental planning, performance planning,* and *broad life planning*. Developmental planning focuses on realistic evaluation of future career options and opportunities, and the creation of activities that will prepare employees for future jobs and career decisions. Performance planning centers on the identification of specific job demand goals, priorities, and reward expectations of current job assignments. Broad life planning involves identifying interests, abilities, experiences, aptitudes, and values that improve self-awareness, self-concept, and career orientations. These activities support organizational career development because they focus on identification of career potential rather than specific roles or careers within a given organization.

It is ultimately the responsibility of employees to develop their own career planning strategy. Employees control decisions such as whether to remain in the organization, accept specific organizational assignments, perform at acceptable levels, or engage in personal growth and developmental activities through learning acquisition and transfer plans. Employees need to construct plans that will enable them to accomplish their career goals, analyze their career potential, and determine whether they possess the skills, competencies, and knowledge necessary to be considered serious candidates for other positions within the organization. Employees must work in concert with managers and supervisors to identify career options and alternatives. This can best be accomplished through performance coaching activities (previously discussed in Chapter 5).

Employee career planning responsibility includes building an awareness of available career opportunities within the organization and identifying those positions that are critical or in great demand. Career opportunity information may be gleaned by networking, conversations with supervisors or HR representatives, organization job postings or manuals, or online postings. A little research allows employees to determine whether they have interest in or sufficient skills required for certain positions. If not, they can arrange for additional training, education, or development in order to be more competitive with fellow employees.

Career planning activities allow employees to analyze their abilities and interests and better match their individual needs for growth and development with those of the organization. Employees must be held responsible for developmental and performance planning actions that will prepare them for challenging career opportunities within the organization. Organizations should use career development activities to promote developmental synergy required for long-term organizational growth.

Organizational career development programs vary in their purpose, approach, ideology, and philosophy. Organizational commitment to transforming employees into their number one asset is absolutely essential to the long-term implementation and success of career development programs. Furthermore, both the individual employee and the organization must benefit from such developmental planning. Therefore, it could be concluded that successful career development programs rely on employees and organizations working together as a team. Organizations must manage programs in such a way that they are continuously identifying and developing career development activities deemed appropriate and sufficient for enhancing employee growth and development. Organizational leaders must indoctrinate managers and supervisors regarding the importance of career development while encouraging employees to become responsible for their own careers.

The amount of time spent and the degree of importance placed on career development determine growth and development of both employees and organizations, The by-product is increased organizational harmony, efficiency, and effectiveness.

ADOPTING A CONTINUOUS CHANGE PHILOSOPHY

One certainty in organizational life is that change is constant. Change best occurs when organizational leaders, managers, and supervisors create an environment conducive for employees to examine their own performance acuity. This activity reveals areas of strengths and weakness, incorporating new approaches to performance growth and development. If employees are encouraged to examine their present performance, determine their strengths and weaknesses, identify growth and development activities, and participate in learning acquisition and transfer, they will be more willing to incorporate new performance behaviors. In this way, organizations encourage and promote continuous reflection on the part of employees, thus putting into motion the concept of *reflection, learning, and practice*, which is essential to the adoption of a continuous change philosophy.

The reflection, learning, and practice cycle fosters continuous improvement. These three simple ingredients are essential to the continued development of competencies, skills, and knowledge, reflecting the ongoing, developmental philosophy of mastery learners who are constantly searching for new awarenesses, insights, and understandings. They force employees to continuously challenge their assumptions and beliefs, compelling them to try new and exciting approaches to learning and development. In support, organizations must become expert at helping their employees reflect on their practices, provide learning and development opportunities, and allow ample time for practice and implementation of new skills and knowledge in the workplace. Then and only then will employees adopt the kind of continuous lifelong learning philosophy that results in mastery.

To adopt a continuous change philosophy, organizations must first accept the responsibility of preparing managers and supervisors for a role in the change process. This strategy includes identifying their responsibilities as well as possible actions to be taken before employees engage in change activities. Managers and supervisors must accept their responsibilities proactively, and embrace and become involved in change.

Second, organizations must help managers develop performance coaching skills, including interpersonal communications strategies and feedback techniques useful in encouraging employees to change behaviors. These developmental performance coaching skills in and of themselves act as a catalyst of change for many managers. Consequently, the reflection, learning, and practice cycle should be incorporated as employees endeavor to integrate new skills and knowledge on the job.

Third, it may be critical to institute cohort work teams to participate in change activities together. These teams take part in change activities as a group and are able to develop a common understanding, language, and context in which change can occur. This, in an indirect way, yields better support and integration of change for team members while fostering improved learning due to consistent handling of common questions and concerns. Cohort work teams also prevent negative peer pressure so common among stagnant, unmotivated employees.

Fourth, organizations should encourage managers to identify and communicate performance standards by which their employees will be judged. These standards serve as the minimum requirements for excellence and can be attached to both performance outputs and performance activities (see Chapter 3). Performance standards provide an atmosphere for employees to review their current skills and knowledge vis-à-vis the job to be done. This analysis could well be the most critical activity in which employees take part while preparing for change. Without this information, employees are unable to measure their performance against that desired by the organization (Gilley & Coffern, 1994).

Fifth, managers should communicate the importance of learning and development to their employees. This strategy helps employees appreciate the time, energy, and effort they will exchange for new skills and knowledge. It also helps employees answer the question, "What's in it for me?" By explaining the importance of learning and development, managers stoke the fires of learning acquisition and encourage practice and reflection that deepen employees' skills and understanding.

Sixth, managers should communicate their support of learning and development, as it is not enough to simply articulate the importance of new skills and knowledge. It is equally important for managers to communicate their willingness to support employees' application of new skills on the job by demonstrating patience with employees during skill acquisition, particularly if performance falls as employees struggle to integrate new skills and knowledge. Management patience fosters a supportive work environment and encourages employees to take risks in improving their performance capacity.

Seventh, organizations should encourage managers to discover and bestow rewards and recognition on employees who acquire new skills and knowledge and subsequently apply them to the job. In Chapter 8, we discussed reward and recognition strategies along with the type of rewards effective in enhancing employee involvement and commitment. Employees must be aware of potential rewards and recognition as an incentive to participate in reflection, learning, and practice activities. In this way, employees are encouraged and conditioned to adopt a continuous change philosophy.

OVERCOMING THE SELF-DEFEATING AND DYSFUNCTIONAL ORGANIZATION

Self-defeating and dysfunctional organizations repeatedly react to crisis situations by suboptimizing themselves. Behavior such as this impedes high performance, causing organizations to be forever lost in a spiral between the *laws of fast forgetting, slow learning,* and *organizational stupidity.*

Organizations experience fast forgetting when their perceived success causes them to forget basic management and organizational principles that were instrumental in bringing about financial and operational prosperity. They become short term-oriented and make unwise decisions in their attempt to maximize market position and profits. They lose sight of reality and fail to consider the contributions and sacrifices that employees have made in order for the organization to succeed. Furthermore, organizations fail to invest in their people or create developmental environments conducive to long-term success. In short, in their attempts to maximize financial gain organizations forget how they became successful, thus fostering self-defeating and dysfunctional behavior.

Many organizations are slow to learn from their mistakes and, consequently, are doomed to repeat them. This condition is referred to as the law of slow learning. Slow learning occurs when managers and leaders fail to adequately understand how their decisions and actions contribute to the organization's shortfalls. By failing to comprehend the circumstances and conditions that lead to crisis situations, organizations are destined to repeat them. Many organizations attempt to minimize their losses by denying the situation or affixing blame on others. As a result, they demonstrate self-defeating and dysfunctional behaviors resulting in high absenteeism, turnover, rising costs, and paranoid work environments.

Some organizations commit the worst sin of all by embracing the law of organizational stupidity. This occurs when organizations perform the same tasks and activities, or make the same decisions over and over again while expecting "different results." In other words, organizations repeatedly bang their heads against the wall, each and every time anticipating that it won't hurt while, much to their surprise, it does! While the simple solution to such behavior is to stop doing what is hurtful, organizations stubbornly insist on repeating tasks, activities, and decisions that produce consistently negative results. This exemplifies classic self-defeating and dysfunctional behavior.

When these three laws are allowed to continue unchecked, they will forever lock organizations into a self-defeating and dysfunctional cycle that is nearly impossible to break. Understanding and addressing self-defeating and dysfunctional behaviors appropriately is one of the few successful means of overcoming this cycle.

According to Hardy and Schwartz (1996), self-defeating and dysfunctional behavior is caused by fear. They contend that organizational fears are emotional responses to outside events that are not filtered through the organization's core beliefs and guiding principles, which should collectively express what the organization does and what purpose it serves. They further assert that there are two types of fear: mythical and realistic. Mythical fears are destructive to organizations because they use these fears to avoid performance improvement strategies. Realistic fears are based on fact, not destructive or paranoid organizational self-talk. Realistic fears can be managed and addressed through proactive actions designed to avoid overreactive, counterproductive responses to unknown or unsubstantiated perceptions.

Beliefs and fears are not the only behaviors that make an organization self-defeating and dysfunctional. The way an organization deals with problems or crises reflects its degree of self-defeating and dysfunctional behavior. Organizations that are reactive (responding without strategically thinking about consequences) are:

- replicating—providing past counterproductive strategies without considering their appropriateness
- cost absorbing—willing to accept high costs for mistakes
- minimizing consequences—denying the seriousness of their situation
- blaming—attempting to identify scapegoats for inappropriate decisions and actions

In short, these organizations are self-defeating and dysfunctional (Hardy & Schwartz, 1996).

Most healthy and capable employees in self-defeating and dysfunctional organizations actively resist counterproductive policies or procedures until they become exhausted and ultimately flee the environment. Other less capable employees either hide within the organization, avoiding conflict, or adapt to the unhealthy environment. These passive behaviors enable many employees to survive counterproductive or pathological environments, but do little to facilitate organizational change or improvement. Moreover, less talented or creative employees become the "organizational bench" while high performers move on to healthier environments where their potential will be maximized.

Overcoming self-defeating and dysfunctional behavior in organizations proves to be a difficult task. Nevertheless, making the transition to developmental organizations is imperative. One suggestion is for organizations to avoid unnecessary and negative self-talk, which can be accomplished by focusing on realistic, supportable, documentable information. In this way, organizations do not rely on unsubstantiated information or mythical fears.

Another strategy organizations may employ is to reflect on their decisions and actions to determine whether they are beneficial or productive. Organizations should discover and abandon those actions or interventions that fail to produce desired results.

Finally, organizations should always remember their pathway to success. By doing so, organizations avoid the trap of fast forgetting and remain focused and consistent during periods of prosperity as well as economic decline. That is, organizations must keep their "eye on the ball" at all times to guarantee continuous, long-term success.

As firms make the transition to developmental organizations, they must remember the importance of their people in the success equation and avoid self-defeating and dysfunctional behaviors by breaking the cycles of fast forgetting, slow learning, and organizational stupidity. They must also recognize when their fears are mythical or realistic, and focus only on healthy fears that can be measured, validated, controlled, and managed. In this way, the energy and effort put forth by organizations can be directed toward a developmental perspective—one that ultimately transforms the organization, causing it to rely on its employees and encourage investment in their ever-increasing talents and abilities. Thus, a developmental organization is created.

CONCLUSION

It is not enough for organizations to adopt a performance alignment process, develop leadership effectiveness, or create virtual teams. They must also adopt strategies that help them make the transformation into developmental organizations—the next step in organizational evolution. Such a transformation involves reinventing the human resource function, linking employees to the organization's strategic business goals and objectives, utilizing the inclusive approach to problem solving, building diversity, adopting career development strategies, embracing a continuous change philosophy, and overcoming self-defeating and dysfunctional behaviors. Adoption of these strategies enables organizations to practice the reflection, learning, and practice philosophies so essential to integrating change as a constant thrust within an organization. When organizations have adopted such an approach they will be able to redefine, reconstruct, and reinvent themselves over and over again. By doing so they will have evolved from the learning organization into the developmental organization.

Appendix

PERFORMANCE COACHING INVENTORY

The Performance Coaching Inventory identifies a manager's perform-ance coaching competencies in seven areas: synergistic relationships, training employees, career counseling, confronting performance , men-toring employees, enhancing employees' self-esteem, and rewarding performance.

Evaluating managers' current performance coaching competencies helps determine their strengths and weaknesses. The Performance Coaching Inventory solicits managers' self-perception as well as em-ployees' perceptions of their managers' strengths and weaknesses, not-ing similarities and differences between both parties' observations.

In order to obtain this information, managers should complete the Performance Coaching Inventory "self-report," (pp. 211–218) while *three* employees complete the "my manager report" (pp. 220–228). The questionnaires require completion pursuant to the instructions below.

Read each question carefully, determine your response, and circle the most appropriate number. The point value for each answer is:

> Never   = 1 point
> Infrequently = 2 points
> Sometimes   = 3 points
> Frequently = 4 points
> Always   = 5 points

Complete the questionnaire. Next, transfer responses from each questionnaire to the *Competency Scoring* sheets (four total, i.e., the man-ager's "self-report" [p. 219] and three employee "my manager reports" [p. 229]). Refer to the *Competency Scoring* sheet for the items statement (identified with numbers) under each of the seven performance coach-ing competencies, which are: *Synergistic Relationships, Training Employees,*

Career Counseling, Confronting Performance, Mentoring Employees, Enhancing Employees' Self-Esteem, and Rewarding Performance.

Enter the point value (1–5 points) on the *Points* line, which is below each of the numbered *Items*. For example, if you responded "Sometimes" to item number 1, then a "3" (point value) would be entered directly below the number 1 on the scoring sheet. Total all points recorded for this competency area and enter the cumulative score on the *total* line. Repeat this process for all seven competency areas.

After calculating the total for each of the seven competency areas, total *all* seven competency areas (total of totals) and enter this overall score at the bottom of the page on the *Performance Coaching Mastery Score* line.

To develop an accurate profile, it will be necessary to obtain an average score for the three employee **"my manager reports,"** for all seven competency areas, and the mastery score.

Once the manager's score and employees' scores have been calculated, transfer them to the *Performance Coaching Competency Scales* (p. 230). Enter the manager's total score for each of the seven competency areas along the appropriate number line. These separate and overall scores provide managers with their perception of current competencies as a performance coach. Repeat this process, in a different color, for the employees' average scores. Now, compare separate and overall manager's scores with those of employees.

Finally, transfer the manager's and employees' average scores from the *Performance Coaching Mastery Score* found at the bottom of the Competency Score Sheet (p. 219 and p. 229) to the *Performance Coaching Pyramid* (p. 231). Comparing these scores allows managers to ascertain given performance coaching aptitudes as compared to employees' perceptions of their skills. This information establishes a baseline for developing a learning acquisition and transfer plan that helps managers overcome their weaknesses while building on strengths.

Performance Coaching Process

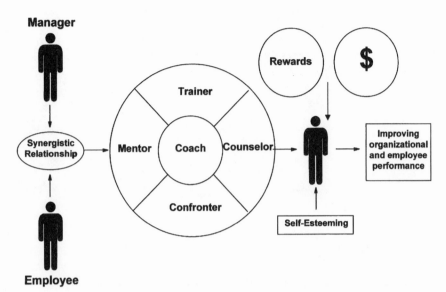

Used by Permission: Gilley, Jerry W., and Boughton, Nathaniel W., *Stop Managing, Start Coaching!* McGraw-Hill, 1996, New York.

MANAGER'S SELF-REPORT

Read each statement carefully and identify the most representative response of your actual behavior as a manager. Circle the most appropriate number provided. Complete the questionnaire.

	Never	Infrequently	Sometimes	Frequently	Always
1. I provide a communication climate that is nonthreatening, comfortable, and conducive for sharing information.	1	2	3	4	5
2. When training employees, I consider carefully the information or material to be presented, and identify its point of contact with their lives, interests, and experiences.	1	2	3	4	5
3. I provide recommendations to employees about their career development needs.	1	2	3	4	5
4. I immediately point out employees' performance shortfalls before they become serious.	1	2	3	4	5
5. I encourage a free exchange of ideas, opinions, and feelings in order to help employees discuss their personal and professional problems.	1	2	3	4	5

	Never	Infre- quently	Some- times	Fre- quently	Always
6. I provide employees oppor- tunities to achieve or ac- complish work that is meaningful to them.	1	2	3	4	5
7. I recognize employees for their overall and specific contributions to improved organizational performance.	1	2	3	4	5
8. I openly communicate with employees to help them improve their job per- formance.	1	2	3	4	5
9. I assign employees work that allows them to apply new skills and competencies on the job.	1	2	3	4	5
10. I help employees consider career options and alter- natives.	1	2	3	4	5
11. I use performance standards or criteria to measure employees' performance.	1	2	3	4	5
12. I share with employees my extensive knowledge of the organization.	1	2	3	4	5
13. I share power and control with employees.	1	2	3	4	5
14. I provide rewards and recog- nition when employees produce long-term results rather than short-term gains.	1	2	3	4	5
15. I encourage interpersonal interaction with employees.	1	2	3	4	5
16. When training employees, I present new information in a practical and meaning- ful manner.	1	2	3	4	5
17. I help employees make career decisions.	1	2	3	4	5

	Never	Infre-quently	Some-times	Fre-quently	Always
18. I clearly communicate the negative consequences of poor performance to employees.	1	2	3	4	5
19. I am willing to be responsible for the growth and development of employees.	1	2	3	4	5
20. I appoint employees to chair committees, task forces or projects where they can have influence over the results achieved.	1	2	3	4	5
21. I reward risk taking and decisive decision making.	1	2	3	4	5
22. I accept employees as unique individuals with differing personalities and inter-personal styles.	1	2	3	4	5
23. When training employees, I present information in a step-by-step manner rather than providing an overview of how a task or job is to be completed.	1	2	3	4	5
24. I pose hypothetical questions to employees to expand their point of view regarding their career.	1	2	3	4	5
25. I confront poor performance in such a way (i.e., using conflict resolution and problem-solving techniques) that employees maintain their self-esteem and dignity.	1	2	3	4	5
26. I am willing to provide information about the mission, goals, and strategic direction of the organization with employees.	1	2	3	4	5

	Never	Infre-quently	Some-times	Fre-quently	Always
27. I attempt to develop a close, personal affiliation with employees.	1	2	3	4	5
28. I celebrate the successes of employees such as promotions, certification designations, and specialized training.	1	2	3	4	5
29. I attempt to get personally involved with my employees.	1	2	3	4	5
30. When training employees, I present only one idea or concept at a time to help them integrate it with their existing knowledge.	1	2	3	4	5
31. I help employees discover the underlying reasons "why" they have selected their current career path.	1	2	3	4	5
32. I provide employees a non-judgmental description of the performance behavior to be changed.	1	2	3	4	5
33. I am willing to serve as a confidant when employees have personal or professional problems.	1	2	3	4	5
34. I encourage employees to act on their personal values and beliefs.	1	2	3	4	5
35. I reward performance that produces the overall results needed by the organization.	1	2	3	4	5
36. I attempt to develop trust with employees.	1	2	3	4	5
37. When training employees, I use feedback and frequent summaries to facilitate retention, recall, and application.	1	2	3	4	5

	Never	Infre-quently	Some-times	Fre-quently	Always
38. I help employees examine the seriousness of their career commitment by posing alternative views for them to consider.	1	2	3	4	5
39. I disclose my feelings about poor performance with employees.	1	2	3	4	5
40. I encourage employees to take risks in order to advance their careers and succeed within the organization.	1	2	3	4	5
41. I encourage employees to participate in decision-making sessions and develop action plans designed to solve problems.	1	2	3	4	5
42. I reward teamwork and cooperation rather than individual contributions and efforts.	1	2	3	4	5
43. I openly and honesty express my opinions of my employees' performance.	1	2	3	4	5
44. When training employees, I provide a familiar frame of reference by presenting new information in terms and symbols that they understand.	1	2	3	4	5
45. I share my own career decisions with employees as a way of helping them think about and carefully examine their career options.	1	2	3	4	5
46. I clarify the effects of poor performance on the organization with employees.	1	2	3	4	5

	Never	Infre-quently	Some-times	Fre-quently	Always
47. I use developmental plans to encourage employees' growth and development.	1	2	3	4	5
48. I share leadership responsibilities with my employees.	1	2	3	4	5
49. I use money and other financial incentives to reward employees for their contributions and efforts.	1	2	3	4	5
50. I attempt to enhance the self-esteem of employers by delegating work assignments that are rewarding and satisfying.	1	2	3	4	5
51. When training employees, I use a variety of instructional methods to arouse their attention and to illustrate specific points.	1	2	3	4	5
52. I express confidence in my employees' abilities to achieve their career goals.	1	2	3	4	5
53. When a conflict occurs with employees, I listen carefully to what they are saying in order to understand their point of view.	1	2	3	4	5
54. I allow employees the opportunity to grow and develop even if it means that other managers will be advising and influencing their career decisions.	1	2	3	4	5
55. I demonstrate a willingness to accept individual differences among employees.	1	2	3	4	5
56. I reward employees when they meet or exceed my expectations.	1	2	3	4	5

	Never	Infre-quently	Some-times	Fre-quently	Always
57. I attempt to enhance the self-esteem of employees even when their perform-ance does not warrant it.	1	2	3	4	5
58. When training employees, I use terms, symbols, and language that they are familiar with.	1	2	3	4	5
59. I ask employees to identify their career goals and to explain their strategy for achieving them.	1	2	3	4	5
60. When a conflict occurs with an employee, I clarify what the employee is saying in order to better understand his or her concerns.	1	2	3	4	5
61. I provide timely feedback of observed performance in order to improve the per-formance of my employees.	1	2	3	4	5
62. I encourage employees to a obtain personal mastery of competency or skill area (i.e., customer service or personal selling).	1	2	3	4	5
63. I make certain employees have the necessary resources and equipment to success-fully complete a task or job.	1	2	3	4	5
64. I help employees improve their knowledge and skills in order to enhance their careers.	1	2	3	4	5
65. When training employees, I arrange the presentation of material so that each step of a task or skill leads easily and naturally to the next.	1	2	3	4	5

	Never	Infre-quently	Some-times	Fre-quently	Always
66. I help employees with their long-term career planning and development.	1	2	3	4	5
67. When a conflict occurs with an employee, I ask non-threatening questions to better understand what he or she is trying to com-municate.	1	2	3	4	5
68. I teach employees how to adjust to the political climate of the organization.	1	2	3	4	5
69. During periods of conflict, I encourage open and honest communications in order to ensure that employees' self-esteem is maintained.	1	2	3	4	5
70. I make certain that employ-ees understand how their job contributes to the success of the organization.	1	2	3	4	5

COMPETENCY SCORING SHEET

Competency 1: Synergistic Relationships

Item:	1,	8,	15,	22,	29,	36,	43,	50,	57,	64,	Total
Points:	—	—	—	—	—	—	—	—	—	—	——

Performance Coaching Role Competencies

Competency 2: Training Employees

Item:	2,	9,	16,	23,	30,	37,	44,	51,	58,	65,	Total
Points:	—	—	—	—	—	—	—	—	—	—	——

Competency 3: Career Counseling

Item:	3,	10,	17,	24,	31,	38,	45,	52,	59,	66,	Total
Points:	—	—	—	—	—	—	—	—	—	—	——

Competency 4: Confronting Performance

Item:	4,	11,	18,	25,	32,	39,	46,	53,	60,	67,	Total
Points:	—	—	—	—	—	—	—	—	—	—	——

Competency 5: Mentoring Employees

Item:	5,	12,	19,	26,	33,	40,	47,	54,	61,	68,	Total
Points:	—	—	—	—	—	—	—	—	—	—	——

Competency 6: Enhancing Employees' Self-Esteem

Item:	6,	13,	20,	27,	34,	41,	48,	55,	62,	69,	Total
Points:	—	—	—	—	—	—	—	—	—	—	——

Competency 7: Rewarding Performance

Item:	7,	14,	21,	28,	35,	42,	49,	56,	63,	70,	Total
Points:	—	—	—	—	—	—	—	—	—	—	——

Performance Coaching Mastery Score   (Total of Totals) ____

70		210	245	280	315	350
20%		60%	70%	80%	90%	100%

MY MANAGER REPORT

Read each statement carefully and identify the most representative response of your manager's actual behavior. Circle the most appropriate number provided. Complete the questionnaire.

	Never	Infre-quently	Some-times	Fre-quently	Always
1. My manager provides a communication climate that is nonthreatening, comfortable, and conducive for sharing information.	1	2	3	4	5
2. When training employees, my manager considers carefully the information or material to be presented, and identifies its point of contact with their lives, interests, and experiences.	1	2	3	4	5
3. My manager provides recommendations to employees about their career development needs.	1	2	3	4	5
4. My manager immediately points out employees' performance shortfalls before they become serious.	1	2	3	4	5
5. My manager encourages a free exchange of ideas, opinions, and feelings in order to help employees discuss their personal and professional problems.	1	2	3	4	5

	Never	Infre-quently	Some-times	Fre-quently	Always
6. My manager provides employees with opportunities to achieve or accomplish work that is meaningful to them.	1	2	3	4	5
7. My manager recognizes employees for their overall and specific contributions to improved organizational performance.	1	2	3	4	5
8. My manager openly communicates with employees to help them improve their job performance.	1	2	3	4	5
9. My manager assigns employees work that allows them to apply new skills and competencies on the job.	1	2	3	4	5
10. My manager helps emloyees consider career options and alternatives.	1	2	3	4	5
11. My manager uses performance standards or criteria to measure employees' performance.	1	2	3	4	5
12. My manager shares with employees his or her extensive knowledge of the organization.	1	2	3	4	5
13. My manager shares power and control with employees.	1	2	3	4	5
14. My manager provides rewards and recognition when employees produce long-term results rather than short-term gains.	1	2	3	4	5
15. My manager encourages interpersonal interaction with employees.	1	2	3	4	5

	Never	Infre-quently	Some-times	Fre-quently	Always
16. When training employees, my manager presents new information in a practical and meaningful manner.	1	2	3	4	5
17. My manager helps employees make career decisions.	1	2	3	4	5
18. My manager clearly communicates the negative consequences of poor performance to employees.	1	2	3	4	5
19. My manager is willing to be responsible for the growth and development of employees.	1	2	3	4	5
20. My manager appoints employees to chair committees, task forces, or projects where they can have influence over the results achieved.	1	2	3	4	5
21. My manager rewards risk taking and decisive decision making.	1	2	3	4	5
22. My manager accepts employees as unique individuals with differing personalities and interpersonal styles.	1	2	3	4	5
23. When training employees, my manager presents information in a step-by-step manner rather than providing an overview of how a task or job is to be completed.	1	2	3	4	5
24. My manager poses hypothetical questions to employees to expand their point of view regarding their career.	1	2	3	4	5

	Never	Infre-quently	Some-times	Fre-quently	Always
25. My manager confronts poor performance in such a way (i.e., using conflict resolution and problem-solving techniques) that employees maintain their self-esteem and dignity.	1	2	3	4	5
26. My manager is willing to provide information about the mission, goals, and strategic direction of the organization with employees.	1	2	3	4	5
27. My manager attempts to develop a close, personal affiliation with employees.	1	2	3	4	5
28. My manager celebrates the successes of employees such as promotions, certification designations, and specialized training.	1	2	3	4	5
29. My manager attempts to get personally involved with employees.	1	2	3	4	5
30. When training employees, my manager presents only one idea or concept at a time in order to help employees better integrate it with their existing knowledge.	1	2	3	4	5
31. My manager helps employees discover the underlying reasons "why" they have selected their current career path.	1	2	3	4	5
32. My manager provides employees a nonjudgmental description of the performance behavior to be changed.	1	2	3	4	5

	Never	Infre-quently	Some-times	Fre-quently	Always
33. My manager is willing to serve as a confidant when employees have personal or professional problems.	1	2	3	4	5
34. My manager encourages employees to act on their personal values and beliefs.	1	2	3	4	5
35. My manager rewards per-formance that produces the overall results needed by the organization.	1	2	3	4	5
36. My manager attempts to develop trust with employees.	1	2	3	4	5
37. When training employees, my manager uses feedback and frequent summaries to facilitate retention, recall, and application.	1	2	3	4	5
38. My manager helps em-ployees examine the seriousness of their career commitment by posing alternative views for them to consider.	1	2	3	4	5
39. My manager discloses his or her feelings about poor performance with employees.	1	2	3	4	5
40. My manager encourages employees to take risks in order to advance their careers and succeed within the organization.	1	2	3	4	5
41. My manager encourages employees to participate in decision-making sessions and develop action plans, designed to solve problems.	1	2	3	4	5

	Never	Infre-quently	Some-times	Fre-quently	Always
42. My manager rewards team-work and cooperation rather than individual contributions and efforts.	1	2	3	4	5
43. My manager openly and honestly expresses his or opinion of employees' performance.	1	2	3	4	5
44. When training employees, my manager presents new information in terms and symbols that are easily understood.	1	2	3	4	5
45. My manager shares his or her own career decisions with employees as a way of helping them carefully examine their career options.	1	2	3	4	5
46. My manager communicates to employees the impact of poor performance on the organization.	1	2	3	4	5
47. My manager uses develop-mental plans to encourage employee growth and development.	1	2	3	4	5
48. My manager shares leader-ship responsibilities with his or her employees.	1	2	3	4	5
49. My manager provides finan-cial incentives to reward employees for their contri-butions and efforts.	1	2	3	4	5
50. My manager attempts to enhance the self-esteem of employees by delegating work assignments that are rewarding and satisfying.	1	2	3	4	5

	Never	Infre-quently	Some-times	Fre-quently	Always
51. When training employees, my manager uses a variety of instructional methods to arouse their attention and illustrate specific points.	1	2	3	4	5
52. My manager expresses confidence in employees' abilities to achieve their career goals.	1	2	3	4	5
53. When a conflict occurs with an employee, my manager listens carefully to what the employee is saying in order to understand her or his point of view.	1	2	3	4	5
54. My manager allows employees the opportunity to grow and develop even if it means that other managers will be advising and influencing their career decisions.	1	2	3	4	5
55. My manager is willing to accept individual differences among employees.	1	2	3	4	5
56. My manager rewards employees when they meet or exceed performance expectations.	1	2	3	4	5
57. My manager attempts to enhance the self-esteem of employees even when their performance does not warrant it.	1	2	3	4	5
58. When training employees, my manager uses terms, symbols, and language that employees understand.	1	2	3	4	5

	Never	Infre-quently	Some-times	Fre-quently	Always
59. My manager asks employees to identify their career goals and to explain their strategy for achieving them.	1	2	3	4	5
60. When a conflict occurs with an employee, my manager clarifies what the employee is saying in order to better understand his or her concerns.	1	2	3	4	5
61. My manager provides timely feedback of observed performance in order to improve employee performance.	1	2	3	4	5
62. My manager encourages employees to obtain personal mastery of a competency or skill area (i.e., customer service or personal selling).	1	2	3	4	5
63. My manager provides employees with the necessary resources and equipment to successfully complete a task or job.	1	2	3	4	5
64. My manager helps employees improve their knowledge and skills in order to enhance their careers.	1	2	3	4	5
65. When training employees, my manager organizes the presentation of material so that each step of a task or skill leads easily and naturally to the next.	1	2	3	4	5

	Never	Infre-quently	Some-times	Fre-quently	Always
66. My manager helps employees with their long-term career planning and development.	1	2	3	4	5
67. When a conflict occurs with an employee, my manager asks nonthreatening questions to better understand what the employee is trying to communicate.	1	2	3	4	5
68. My manager teaches employees how to adjust to the political climate of the organization.	1	2	3	4	5
69. During periods of conflict, my manager encourages open and honest communications in order to ensure that employees' self-esteem is maintained.	1	2	3	4	5
70. My manager makes certain that employees understand how their jobs contribute to the success of the organization.	1	2	3	4	5

COMPETENCY SCORING SHEET

Competency 1: Synergistic Relationships

Item:	1,	8,	15,	22,	29,	36,	43,	50,	57,	64,	Total
Points:	__	__	__	__	__	__	__	__	__	__	___

Performance Coaching Role Competencies

Competency 2: Training Employees

Item:	2,	9,	16,	23,	30,	37,	44,	51,	58,	65,	Total
Points:	__	__	__	__	__	__	__	__	__	__	___

Competency 3: Career Counseling

Item:	3,	10,	17,	24,	31,	38,	45,	52,	59,	66,	Total
Points:	__	__	__	__	__	__	__	__	__	__	___

Competency 4: Confronting Performance

Item:	4,	11,	18,	25,	32,	39,	46,	53,	60,	67,	Total
Points:	__	__	__	__	__	__	__	__	__	__	___

Competency 5: Mentoring Employees

Item:	5,	12,	19,	26,	33,	40,	47,	54,	61,	68,	Total
Points:	__	__	__	__	__	__	__	__	__	__	___

Competency 6: Enhancing Employees' Self-Esteem

Item:	6,	13,	20,	27,	34,	41,	48,	55,	62,	69,	Total
Points:	__	__	__	__	__	__	__	__	__	__	___

Competency 7: Rewarding Performance

Item:	7,	14,	21,	28,	35,	42,	49,	56,	63,	70,	Total
Points:	__	__	__	__	__	__	__	__	__	__	___

Performance Coaching Mastery Score   (Total of Totals) ____

70		210	245	280	315	350
20%		60%	70%	80%	90%	100%

Performance Coaching Competency Scales

Synergistic Relationships

| 10 | 20 | 30 | 40 | 50 |

Performace Coaching Role Competencies

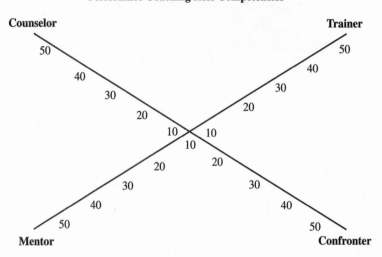

Enhancing Employee Self-Esteem

| 10 | 20 | 30 | 40 | 50 |

Rewarding Performance

| 10 | 20 | 30 | 40 | 50 |

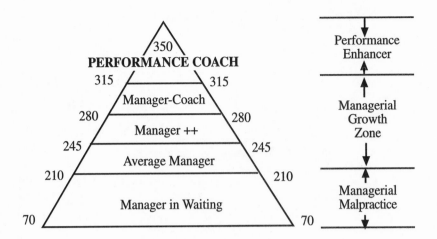

Performance Coaching Pyramid

References

Beatty, R. W. (1989). "Competitive human resource advantage through strategic management of performance." *Human Resource Planning 12* (3): 179–194.

Bolton, R. (1986). *People skills: How to assert yourself, listen to others, and resolve conflicts.* New York: Simon & Schuster.

Bradshaw, P. (1981). *The management of self-esteem: How people can feel good about themselves and better about their organizations.* Englewood Cliffs: Prentice-Hall.

Carlisle, K. E., & Murphy, S. E. (1996). *Practical motivation handbook.* New York: John Wiley & Sons.

Carlson, J. (1987). *Moments of truth: New strategies for today's customer-driven economy.* New York: HarperCollins.

Clifton, D. O., & Nelson, P. (1992). *Soar with your strengths.* New York: Delacorte.

Flannery, T. P., Hofrichter, D. A., & Platten, P. E. (1996). *People performance and pay: Dynamic compensation for changing organizations.* New York: The Free Press.

Gilley, J. W. (1985). "Two myths and managerial theories." *Quality Circles Digest 5* (7): 42–48.

Gilley, J. W. (1998). *Improving HRD practice.* Malabar, FL: Krieger.

Gilley, J. W., & Boughton, N. W. (1996). *Stop managing, start coaching: How performance coaching can enhance commitment and improve productivity.* New York: McGraw-Hill.

Gilley, J. W., & Coffern, A. J. (1994). *Internal consulting for HRD professionals: Tools, techniques, and strategies for improving organizational performance.* New York: McGraw-Hill.

Gilley, J. W., & Davidson, J. (1993). *Quality leadership.* New York: William M. Mercer.

Gilley, J. W., & Eggland, S. A. (1989). *Principles of HRD.* Reading, MA: Perseus Books.

Gilley, J. W., & Eggland, S. A. (1992). *Marketing HRD programs within the organization: Improving the visibility, credibility, and image of programs.* San Francisco: Jossey-Bass.

Gilley, J. W., & Galbraith, M. W. (1984). "A model relationship." *Quality Circles Digest 4* (8): 46–51.

Gilley, J. W., & Marquart, S. (1994). *Performance through people.* New York: William M. Mercer, Inc.

Gilley, J. W., & Maycunich, A. (1998). *Strategically integrated HRD: Partnering to maximize organizational performance.* Reading, MA: Perseus Books.

Goleman, D. (1994). Emotional intelligence: Why it can matter more than IQ. New York: Bantam Books.

Hardy, R. E., & Schwartz, R. (1996). *The self-defeating organization: How smart companies can stop outsmarting themselves.* Reading, MA: Perseus Books.

Katzenbach, J. R., & Smith, D. K. (1994). *The wisdom of teams: Creating the high performance organization.* New York: Harper Business.

Kirkpatrick, D. L. (1985). *How to improve performance through appraisal and coaching.* New York: AMACOM.

Larson, C. E., & LaFasto, F. M. (1989). *Teamwork: What must go right/what can go wrong.* Newbury Park, CA: Sage.

Lawrence, C. (1998). Using executive coaching to accelerate just-in-time learning at fidelity investments. In the proceedings of the *Fast Development for Fast Companies Conference.* San Francisco, CA, 1, 1–8.

LeBoeuf, M. (1985). *Getting results: The secret to motivating yourself and others.* New York: Berkley.

Odiorne, G. (1965). *Management by objectives.* New York: Pittman.

Patterson, J. (1997). *Coming clean about organizational change.* Arlington, VA: American Association of School Administrators.

Peterson, D. B., & Hicks, M. D. (1996). *Development first: Strategies for self-development.* Minneapolis, MN: Personnel Decisions International.

Rogers, C. (1961). *On becoming a person.* Boston: Houghton Mifflin.

Rummler, G. A., & Brache, A. P. (1995). *Improving performance: How to manage the white spaces on the organizational chart.* San Francisco: Jossey-Bass.

Williams, P. (1997). *The magic of teamwork: Proven principles for building winning teams.* Nashville: Thomas Nelson.

Witherspoon, R., & White, R. P. (1997). *Four essential ways that coaching can help executives.* Greensboro, NC: Center for Creative Leadership.

Index